CW01011322

Key TO SUCCESS ON THE *TOEFL*®

Oxford University Press

200 Madison Avenue
New York, NY 10016 USA

Walton Street
Oxford OX2 6DP England

OXFORD is a trademark of Oxford University Press.

Library of Congress Cataloging-in-Publication Data

Feare, Ronald E.
   Key to success on the TOEFL/Ronald E. Feare.
      p. cm.
   ISBN 0-19-434278-6 (student book),—ISBN 0-19-434351-0
(cassette)
   1. English language—Textbooks for foreign speakers. 2. English
language—Examinations, questions, etc.   I. Title.
PE1128.F34   1989   89-16022
428.2'4'076—dc20   CIP

Copyright © 1989 by Oxford University Press, Inc.

All rights reserved. No part of this publication may be reproduced, stored in a
retrieval system, or transmitted, in any form or by any means, electronic,
mechanical, photocopying, recording, or otherwise, without the prior permission
of Oxford University Press.

This book is sold subject to the condition that it shall not, by way of trade or
otherwise, be lent, resold, hired out, or otherwise circulated without the
publisher's prior consent in any form of binding or cover other than that in which
it is published and without a similar condition including this condition being
imposed on the subsequent purchaser.

Editor: Mary Lynne Nielsen
Design Manager: Lynn Luchetti
Production Coordinator: Nora Wertz

Cover design by Kenny Beck.
Graphics by Alan Barnett.

Printing (last digit):   10 9 8 7 6 5 4 3 2 1

Printed in Hong Kong.

Key TO SUCCESS ON THE *TOEFL*®

RONALD E. FEARE

Oxford University Press
1989

CONTENTS

PREFACE

What Is the TOEFL®?

TOEFL® stands for Test of English as a Foreign Language. Since 1963 it has been used by a majority of U.S. colleges and universities as a measure of English ability and readiness for academic study. It is also used by educational institutions in other English-speaking countries.

In addition, scholarship agencies such as the Fulbright depend on the TOEFL® to determine the English proficiency of candidates. Some international businesses require employees to take the TOEFL to demonstrate their knowledge of English.

The TOEFL is easily the most common and well-known test of English. No other language examination comes close to having the importance of the TOEFL in today's world.

Why Use This TOEFL Handbook?

To answer this question, it is important to consider how this handbook is different from most other TOEFL preparation guides.

First, the handbook is the result of many years of careful research and development. Real TOEFL tests were examined in great detail to determine the important elements. This handbook has been used in actual TOEFL preparation classes and has been improved many times.

Second, it explains the TOEFL by giving numerous examples. This means that you will constantly see the kind of material you can expect when you take the test.

Third, it concentrates on the skills and strategies required for the TOEFL. Your success does not depend only on your knowledge of English; it depends also on how good you are at taking tests like the TOEFL.

Fourth, it contains examples and practice tests that "feel like" the TOEFL. The material is written in the same style and has the same type of content as real TOEFL exams.

Finally, it presents the material clearly and efficiently. The assumption is that you are a busy person and that you must prepare for the TOEFL quickly. Using this handbook will definitely save you valuable time.

How Should I Use This Handbook?

If you are just starting to prepare for the TOEFL, you should work from the beginning of the handbook. First read this Preface to familiarize yourself with the test. Then do the entire Listening Comprehension section before moving on to the next section (Structure and Written Expression). You should study all the examples and explanations in each section before you take any practice exercises or practice tests.

If you have already done some preparation for the TOEFL and have taken the test one or more time(s), then you probably want to study the section that seems most difficult for you. In this case, you should go directly to that section and study it first. Again, it is important to study the examples and explanations carefully before taking any practice exercises or practice tests.

At various places in the handbook, you are referred to additional material in the Appendices. The material is in a separate section so that it can be presented and discussed more thoroughly. You should study this material as it is brought to your attention. Don't think that it is less important because it is at the end.

It would be a good idea for you to study two sections of the Appendices as soon as possible: "Ways to Improve Your Listening Ability" in Appendix A (page 133) and "Ways to Improve Your Reading Ability and Vocabulary" in Appendix C (page 153). You can start improving in these areas now by following the advice in these two sections.

There are the equivalent of three TOEFL examinations in this handbook. Two of these exams are used for practice exercises and practice tests. You will be taking these as you study each section of the TOEFL. The final TOEFL exam should be taken only after you have done all practice exercises and tests.

It is very important for you to follow these guidelines if you want to obtain the most benefit from the material in this handbook.

How Is the TOEFL Organized?

The TOEFL always has three major sections: Listening Comprehension, Structure and Written Expression, and Vocabulary and Reading Comprehension. These three sections are briefly described below.

Each section is in multiple-choice format. This means that you are given four possible answers, and you must choose the most appropriate one.

Section 1 Listening Comprehension (administered by cassette)

Single Statements (Part A)
You will listen to a series of single sentences on the cassette. For each sentence, you will choose the answer that has the closest meaning to the sentence you heard.

Short Conversations (Part B)
You will listen to several short conversations between two speakers on the cassette. Each conversation is followed by a question about what the speakers said.

Academic Talks and Long Conversations (Part C)
You will listen to academic talks and longer conversations on the cassette. Each conversation or talk is followed by several questions about it.

A cassette symbol appears before those sections with which the cassette is used.

Section 2 Structure and Written Expression

Structure
You will read sentences in which some words are missing. Only one answer completes each sentence properly.

Written Expression
You will read sentences that have four underlined parts. You will choose the part that is incorrect in formal written English.

Section 3 Vocabulary and Reading Comprehension

Vocabulary
You will read sentences having an underlined word or phrase. You will choose the answer that has the closest meaning to the underlined word or phrase.

Reading Comprehension
You will read several passages on various academic topics. Each passage is followed by several questions about it.

NOTE: A new writing section has been added to the TOEFL exams given in March, May, September, and October. Your result in this section is given as a separate score. Your overall TOEFL score for the three major sections is not affected. More information on the writing section can be found later in this handbook.

What Are the Types of the TOEFL?

There are two major types of the TOEFL exam: the International TOEFL and the Special TOEFL. The International TOEFL is given six times a year in over 130 countries and is administered on Saturday mornings. The Special TOEFL is also given six times a year, but in less than half as many countries, and is administered on Friday afternoons.

Both exams have the same sections and parts listed previously. However, it is more expensive to take the Special TOEFL because it is given at a limited number of institutions.

How Long Is the TOEFL?

The TOEFL comes in two different lengths—the short form and the long form.

Short Form

The short form consists of 150 questions and takes about one-and-a-half hours to complete. (An additional hour is required for admitting people, completing identification material, and distributing and collecting the tests.)

Section	Time	Number of Questions
Listening Comprehension	30 minutes	50 questions
Structure and Written Expression	25 minutes	40 questions
Vocabulary and Reading Comprehension	45 minutes	60 questions

At the present time, the short form will probably be given in the following months: February, March, May, September, and October. For other months, the form may be either short or long.

Long Form

The long form consists of 230 questions and takes over two hours to complete. (An additional hour is required for administrative matters.)

Section	Time	Number of Questions
Listening Comprehension	40 minutes	80 questions
Structure and Written Expression	35 minutes	60 questions
Vocabulary and Reading Comprehension	65 minutes	90 questions

The long form is basically a short form that has 80 extra questions. These extra questions do not count as part of your TOEFL score. They are experimental questions that are being checked for use on future TOEFL exams. There is no way for you to know which questions are really being tested and which are experimental.

At the present time, the long form may be given in any of the following months: January, April, June, July, August, November, and December. However, there is no way of knowing in advance whether the short form or the long form will be used in these months. Also, there is no correlation between the type of TOEFL (that is, international or special) and the length of the exam.

What Is a Good Score on the TOEFL?

This is a difficult question to answer because universities and colleges vary greatly in the score they require of applicants. In general, a score below 400 is not good, and a score above 600 is excellent. (The maximum score on any TOEFL is 677.)

The following table gives a general indication of the type of score you may need for U.S. educational institutions.

Institution	Score Range	Average Score
2-year college or technical school	400–500	450
4-year undergraduate college or university	450–550	500
2–3 year graduate college or university	500–600	550

Some colleges and universities do not require a TOEFL score for admission. In these cases, however, you generally have to take an English placement test. If your score is not adequate, then you have to enroll in the school's intensive English program.

How Can I Register for the TOEFL?

The *Bulletin of Information for TOEFL* contains registration forms and additional information about the TOEFL. It can be obtained by writing to:

TOEFL Services
CN 6151
Princeton, NJ 08541-6151
USA

In the United States, most admissions offices of colleges and universities, as well as intensive English programs, have the *Bulletin of Information for TOEFL.*

Outside of the United States, you should contact the Cultural Affairs Officer of the U.S. Information Service in your country. You may also write to the address above.

General Test-Taking Strategies

In this handbook you will learn the important test-taking strategies for each section of the TOEFL. The general strategies below are useful for all sections of the TOEFL.

- Do not read the instructions that begin each part of the TOEFL. The instructions, as well as the examples, are the same from test to test. Check quickly to make sure the format of the test has not been changed (this is very unlikely) and then move on to the questions.

NOTE: The wording of the instructions in this handbook differs slightly from that of the actual TOEFL. However, the format of all the tests and exercises in this handbook is identical to the TOEFL.

- When you answer questions, follow these three basic steps:

  1. Look for the correct answer. If you are certain of it, mark the answer on your answer sheet.
  2. If you are not certain, check quickly for the answers that seem impossible. This step may help you find the correct one.
  3. If you are still unsure of the correct answer, guess from the possible correct answers.

- There is NO penalty for guessing, so never leave any blanks on your answer sheet. When guessing, use the same letter choice throughout the exam. [That is, if you guess (B), use (B) throughout the exam. You have a better chance of making correct guesses than if you constantly change the letter you use.]

- Avoid translating from English into your native language. This wastes time and can often confuse you.

The following strategies are useful for Section 2 (Structure and Written Expression) and Section 3 (Vocabulary and Reading Comprehension).

- Take a watch and keep careful track of the time. Remember how long you have to complete each section and to answer each question. (This information is given to you in this text as each section of the TOEFL is discussed.)

- Don't waste any time. You shouldn't rush through the text, but you also shouldn't spend too long on any one question.

- Writing in the TOEFL test booklet is not allowed, but of course you can write on the answer sheet. Here is one trick for you: If you are not sure of an answer and want to go back to it later, you can LIGHTLY put a small checkmark (✔) in the margin of the answer sheet next to the number of the question. Be certain to erase all checkmarks on your answer sheet before the test is finished.

LISTENING COMPREHENSION

The first section of the TOEFL exam tests your ability to understand spoken English. Both the long-form and short-form versions (described in the Preface) contain three parts:

Single Statements (Part A)
Short Conversations (Part B)
Academic Talks and Long Conversations (Part C)

The short-form TOEFL has 50 questions and takes about 30 minutes to complete. The long-form TOEFL has 80 questions and takes about 45 minutes. The listening comprehension section is administered by audiotape.

To do well on this section, you must have good listening skills in English. You can improve your listening ability by talking to native speakers of English frequently, by listening to English broadcasts on television and radio, and by using the telephone as a tool for obtaining information. If you have not already done so, you should review the suggestions in Appendix A (page 133).

Single Statements (Part A)

In Part A, you hear a single, short statement ONLY ONE TIME. You have 12 seconds to choose the correct answer. The correct answer is the one that is CLOSEST IN MEANING to the statement you hear.

MODEL

You will hear: When the speaker finished, she received a big hand.

You will read: (A) The speaker was known for her big hands.
           (B) The speaker finished when she got a big hand.
           (C) The speaker was Finnish.
           (D) The audience applauded the speaker.

(A) This answer is incorrect. You hear *a big hand*, which is an idiom meaning *applause*. However, this idiom does not refer to the size of the speaker's hands.
(B) This answer is incorrect. It has most of the same information, but the order of events is opposite.
(C) This answer is incorrect. You hear *finished* but read *Finnish*. The similar sound could confuse you.
(D) This answer is correct. The idiom *a big hand* means *applause*. The situation suggests that there is an audience.

1

Types of Statements

Below are some general facts that you should know about the kinds of statements in Part A.

- Most statements you hear and the answer choices you read are DECLARATIVE SENTENCES. This means that they are not question forms.

    1. You will hear: Bob tried to do it several times.

        You will read: (A) Bob had several things to do.
        (B) Bob made many attempts to do it.
        (C) Bob tried to change the time.
        (D) Bob had enough time to do it.

        All the sentences above are declarative ones. (B) is correct because it is closest in meaning to what you hear.

- Real question forms are not often used in Part A. However, sometimes a TAG QUESTION is added to a declarative sentence.

    2. You will hear: It was an excellent film, wasn't it?

        You will read: (A) It wasn't an excellent film.
        (B) I need to buy some more film.
        (C) The movie was very good.
        (D) The seller lent the film to me.

        A tag question is used to determine if another person agrees with an idea. The correct answer usually does not have a tag question. (C) has the same meaning as the statement.

- Sometimes an EXCLAMATORY FORM will appear in Part A. Such forms begin with *how* or *what* and end with an exclamation point (!).

    3. You will hear: What a mistake they made!

        You will read: (A) They made a big mess.
        (B) I made them take the water.
        (C) The mistake was made yesterday.
        (D) They made a bad mistake.

        The exclamatory form emphasizes that the mistake was a serious one. (D) is the correct answer.

- Statements containing NEGATIVE WORDS or having NEGATIVE MEANING are common.

    4. You will hear: I don't believe Sue's arrived yet.

        You will read: (A) Sue has to leave soon.
        (B) I believe she's survived the accident.
        (C) I don't think Sue's come yet.
        (D) I don't want to sue her.

        The word *not* makes the statement negative. (C) is the correct answer because *think* means *believe* and *come* means *arrive*.

2

5. You will hear: Mary doubts that she can take a vacation.

   You will read: (A) Mary is not certain she can go on vacation.
   (B) Mary doubts that her vacation will be fun.
   (C) Mary has to find a new vocation.
   (D) Mary has to take a vacation this week.

The word *doubt* has the negative meaning of *not to be certain*. Since *go on vacation* means *take a vacation*, (A) is the correct answer.

• Statements containing TIME EXPRESSIONS and expressing TIME RELATIONSHIPS often occur.

6. You will hear: Tom's parents are leaving the day after tomorrow.

   You will read: (A) Tom's parents are leaving tomorrow.
   (B) Tom's parents are departing in two days.
   (C) Tom's left his pants at the laundry.
   (D) Tom is leaving with his parents tomorrow.

The time expression *day after tomorrow* means the same as *in two days*. *To leave* is the same as *to depart*, so (B) is the correct answer.

7. You will hear: The exam began when the teacher finished reviewing.

   You will read: (A) The exam ended before the review.
   (B) The test started after the review.
   (C) The teacher reviewed the exam with the class.
   (D) The test ended when the review began.

Words and phrases like *when, while, before, after*, and *as soon as* are used to show time relationships. (B) is correct because it maintains the same time relationship as the statement.

• Statements that show CONTRAST with *but* and *although* can occur.

8. You will hear: She used to share a dorm room, but now she doesn't.

   You will read: (A) She is used to sharing a dorm room.
   (B) She is sure that the dorm has room for her.
   (C) Although she has her own room now, she used to share one.
   (D) She must move out of the dorm.

The word *but* shows that there is a contrast between the past and the present. (C) is the correct answer because *although* maintains the same contrast.

• Statements that show CONDITION with *if* and *unless* can occur.

9. You will hear: If you don't register early, you won't get the class you want.

   You will read: (A) You should want to go to class.
   (B) Early registration is not possible.
   (C) You should register when you go to class.
   (D) Unless you register early, you won't get that class.

The negative condition in the *if* clause is used to show some possible future situation. (D) is the correct answer because it maintains the same meaning by using *unless*.

- Statements that show REASON (*because*) and RESULT (*so*) can appear.

10. You will hear: I don't trust him at all because he lied to me.

   You will read: (A) He told me a lie, so I have no faith in him.
   (B) I lied to him because I don't trust him.
   (C) He said the car had no rust at all.
   (D) Everything he says is a lie.

   A relationship of reason (*because*) can be restated in terms of a relationship of result (*so*). (A) maintains the same meaning as the statement.

Types of Correct Answer Choices

For each statement in Part A, there is only one correct answer. This answer is always the one that is CLOSEST IN MEANING to the statement you hear. The types of correct answer choices are described below.

- Sometimes the correct answer is an INFERENCE. An inference is a conclusion you must make from some information. The correct answer is not directly stated; it is only suggested.

11. You will hear: Kyle fixed dessert before making the main dish.

   You will read: (A) Kyle was putting dessert on the table.
   (B) Kyle was preparing a meal.
   (C) Kyle was fixing a plate.
   (D) Kyle was dishing out the dessert.

   From the statement you can conclude that Kyle was cooking. Therefore, (B) is an appropriate inference to make.

- Usually the correct answer is a PARAPHRASE of what you hear. The answer contains all or part of the same information as the statement; it never contains any new information. A paraphrase is also called a RESTATEMENT.

12. You will hear: Carl put on his jacket because of the cold.

   You will read: (A) Carl wore his jacket because he had a cold.
   (B) Because it was chilly, Carl wore his jacket.
   (C) Carl put his jacket on the counter.
   (D) Carl's jacket felt quite cold.

   (B) is the correct paraphrase. It contains all the same information as the statement, even though some of the vocabulary has changed.

13. You will hear: Mike saw me at the supermarket and thought that I was shopping for groceries.

   You will read: (A) Mike and I were shopping for groceries.
   (B) I might shop at the supermarket tomorrow.
   (C) Mike believed I was buying food.
   (D) I didn't notice Mike buying groceries.

   (C) is the correct paraphrase, even though it includes only the last part of the statement and the vocabulary is very different.

4

Strategies for Paraphrasing

One key to success in Part A is knowing how to choose the best PARAPHRASE, or restatement, of the sentence you hear. Below are some important strategies to remember.

- Determine the IMPORTANT IDEAS in the statement you hear. A paraphrase doesn't have to contain all of the same information as the statement.

  14. You will hear: On the top of page 60 is the exercise you need to do for homework.

      You will read: (A) Your homework is on page 60.
      (B) It isn't necessary to do your homework.
      (C) You can do your homework in 60 minutes.
      (D) You need to do all of page 60 for homework.

      The important ideas in the statement are WHAT has to be done and WHERE it is. The correct answer is (A).

- As you listen to a statement, concentrate on the meaning and try to think of other ways of expressing the same meaning. Words that have the same meaning are called SYNONYMS.

  15. You will hear: I'm unable to locate the keys to my car.

      You will read: (A) I think that my keys are in the car.
      (B) We ate some cheese in the car.
      (C) The car is located in the parking lot.
      (D) I can't find my car keys.

      The statement can be rephrased in this way: *unable to* means *can't*, *locate* means *find*, and *keys to the car* means *car keys*. (D) is the correct answer.

- Watch for IDIOMATIC EXPRESSIONS that have special meanings.

  16. You will hear: Phil's feeling under the weather this week.

      You will read: (A) Phil feels sick this week.
      (B) Phil doesn't like the weather.
      (C) Phil is too weak to come.
      (D) Phil did it in under a week.

      The idiom *under the weather* means *sick*. It has a special meaning that cannot be understood from looking at the words in the idiom. (A) is correct.

  Idiomatic expressions are important in all three parts of the Listening Comprehension section. You should study the common idiomatic expressions explained in Appendix A (page 133).

Types of Wrong Answer Choices

The wrong answer choices are designed to confuse you. Some are CLOSE in meaning to what you hear. Others are OPPOSITE or NOT RELATED to what you hear. Since you only have 12 seconds between statements, how can you know which choices to avoid? Here are some ideas.

5

- Be careful of words that are pronounced the same but are spelled differently (called MINIMAL PAIRS).

17. You will hear: Let me know whether Bill is coming.

    You will read: (A) Bill's coming because the weather is good.
    (B) I have no idea when Bill is coming.
    (C) Several bills have come in the mail recently.
    (D) Please tell me if Bill will come.

    In (A), *whether* is pronounced the same as *weather*. In (B), *no* sounds the same as *know*. In (C), *bill* is pronounced the same as the proper name *Bill*. (D) is the correct answer.

- Be careful of words and phrases that SOUND ALIKE but do not have the same meaning.

18. You will hear: Doris took it to the closet.

    You will read: (A) I told Doris to close it.
    (B) I took the doors off the closet.
    (C) Doris clipped the dog's claws.
    (D) Doris put it in the cabinet.

    In (A), *close it* sounds like *closet*. In (B), *doors* sounds like *Doris*. In (C), *claws* sounds like the first syllable in *closet*. Only (D), the correct answer, does not have a sound-alike word to confuse you.

- Be careful of words with MULTIPLE MEANINGS. A word you hear may have an inappropriate meaning in one of the wrong answers.

19. You will hear: He trained hard for the sports meet.

    You will read: (A) Playing sports is hard for him.
    (B) The train was headed for the sports meet.
    (C) He wanted to meet the sports trainer.
    (D) He prepared well for the sports event.

    In (A), *hard* means *difficult*; in (B), *train* is a vehicle; in (C), *meet* means *contact*. However, in the statement you hear, *train* means *prepare*, *hard* means *well*, and *meet* means *event*. Therefore, (D) is the correct answer.

You should have noticed that, in all of these examples, the correct answer is most likely the one that contains SYNONYMS of the words in the statement you hear. The incorrect choices are probably the ones that contain words that sound the same as the words in the statement you hear, but do not have the same meaning.

Previewing the Answers

- Part A begins with about two minutes of directions. The directions are basically the same from test to test (even the examples are the same), so it is not necessary to listen to them or to read them in the test booklet. Instead, you may be able to preview some of the answer sets.

- If the directions for Part A are on the left-hand side of the test booklet, you can preview several of the answer sets on the right-hand side. If the directions are on the right-hand side of the test booklet, then it is not possible to preview the answers. The reason is that you are not allowed to turn the page of the test booklet while the directions are being given.

- When you preview, try to determine the information you expect to hear in each statement.

20. You will read: (A) The package was delivered on time.
(B) He wasn't able to pack it properly.
(C) He shipped the box special delivery.
(D) The package was damaged in flight.

You could expect the statement to be about some kind of package and the way it was mailed.

- If it is possible to do so, you should be able to preview four to eight sets of answer choices. Of course, the exact number will depend on how quickly you are able to read.

- Another chance to preview is BETWEEN STATEMENTS. After you choose the answer for one statement, you may have one to four seconds before you hear the next statement. Use this time to look at the next set of answer choices.

The ability to preview effectively is a very important factor in determining your success in all three parts of the Listening Comprehension section. If you have some idea of what you will hear, it will be much easier for you to choose the correct answer.

Listening Practice A

The audio cassette is necessary to do this section. In the following exercise, you should try to use the strategies you have just learned for Part A. These include:

1. previewing answer sets between statements and, if possible, during the directions;
2. concentrating on the important ideas in each statement you hear;
3. rephrasing what you hear by using synonyms;
4. watching for idiomatic expressions; and
5. being careful of answers containing sound-alike words or phrases, words with multiple meanings, and minimal pairs.

Part A

Directions: In Part A, you will hear a short statement. This statement is spoken just once. It is not written for you, so you must listen carefully to understand its meaning.

After you hear the statement, you will read four possible answers. You must choose the answer that is CLOSEST IN MEANING to the statement you hear. You will then mark the correct answer on your answer sheet.

Example I

You will hear:

You will read: (A) Tom's friend was all right.
(B) Tom and his friend had a long argument.
(C) Tom glued the end to the light.
(D) Tom spent the night alone.

You heard, "Tom argued with his friend all night." Sentence (B), "Tom and his friend had a long argument," has the closest meaning. You should mark (B) on your answer sheet.

Example II

You will hear:

You will read: (A) Can you help me review the exam?
(B) What time is the test?
(C) I don't have time to bring the test.
(D) Can I go to the test right now?

You heard, "Do you have time to go over the test with me?" Sentence (A), "Can you help me review the exam?" has the closest meaning. You should mark (A) on your answer sheet.

GO ON TO THE NEXT PAGE ➤

1. (A) Jane will get her diploma next month.
   (B) Jane hasn't seen her diploma yet.
   (C) Jane was given her diploma a month ago.
   (D) Jane couldn't get her diploma last month.

2. (A) The tests will probably be corrected by midday.
   (B) None of the exams can be scored by noon.
   (C) The exams will be crated for shipment soon.
   (D) The tests have already been corrected.

3. (A) Your parents will visit us for a while.
   (B) Let's take a minute to prance through the park.
   (C) Your folks were here a few minutes ago.
   (D) I'd like to visit your parents briefly.

4. (A) She's probably wondering where he is.
   (B) He's quite a fine person.
   (C) What a wonderful prize he won!
   (D) I wonder what person he meant.

5. (A) The party wasn't for Jim or Mary.
   (B) Neither Jim nor Mary went to the party.
   (C) Mary needed to meet Jim at the party.
   (D) Jim couldn't help Mary prepare for the party.

6. (A) The politician's attitude annoyed the reporter.
   (B) The political leader reported her to the authorities.
   (C) The politician was bothered by the journalist's questions.
   (D) The reporter asked the politician important questions.

7. (A) You shouldn't have told me a lie.
   (B) You shouldn't have lied about the fare.
   (C) I think it's fair to relieve me.
   (D) You shouldn't lie down on the floor.

8. (A) We got there after all the seats were sold.
   (B) We wanted good places to sit.
   (C) We adjusted the seats when we arrived.
   (D) The new seats have just arrived.

9. (A) I can't think about this problem right now.
   (B) This problem seems unsolvable to me.
   (C) This isn't the right answer, is it?
   (D) Anyone can solve this problem.

10. (A) It ought to be expensive.
    (B) It shouldn't be so cheap.
    (C) It looks like an inexpensive automobile.
    (D) It costs more than it should.

11. (A) The holiday was over by the time our guests arrived.
    (B) We guessed that several people would come.
    (C) Several people visited us during the holidays.
    (D) We were guests at our friend's house.

GO ON TO THE NEXT PAGE ➤

12. (A) She almost never eats vegetables.
    (B) She sells vegetables for a living.
    (C) She enjoys eating vegetables.
    (D) She has fun growing vegetables.

13. (A) I had some problems with my heart.
    (B) I was glad to get a new oak chest.
    (C) When I discussed my situation, I felt better.
    (D) I had problems playing chess.

14. (A) The beef at that store is excellent.
    (B) I think it's better that we meet at the market.
    (C) The meat used to be better.
    (D) I bet her that there wasn't any meat at the store.

15. (A) Barry reached my home in time.
    (B) Barry was unable to reach me at work.
    (C) He reached me several times.
    (D) He failed to contact me at all.

16. (A) Pete doesn't care about us very much.
    (B) I don't think Pete's very careful.
    (C) I think Les gave the purse to Carla.
    (D) Pete's son cares for him a lot.

17. (A) The water glasses were dirty.
    (B) Washing her glasses improved her vision.
    (C) She watered the grass so it would grow better.
    (D) She can't see well without her glasses.

18. (A) He wouldn't give me anything.
    (B) Each day he gave me some of his time.
    (C) He didn't pay any attention to me.
    (D) He didn't know what time it was.

19. (A) I've been told that the lecturer is quite energetic.
    (B) The loudspeaker is known for its dynamic sound.
    (C) I can't understand what the lecturer is talking about.
    (D) Today I heard a dynamic speech at the university.

20. (A) I've been off for two months.
    (B) I can't get used to this warm weather.
    (C) It doesn't seem like spring weather.
    (D) It's already been summer for two months.

  STOP

11

Transcript and Answers for Listening Practice A

Example I Tom argued with his friend all night.
Example II Do you have time to go over the test with me?

1. Jane received her diploma last month.
2. The tests should be corrected by noon.
3. Let's visit your parents for a few minutes.
4. What a wonderul person he is!
5. Mary didn't come to the party, and Jim didn't either.
6. The important political leader was annoyed by the reporter's questions.
7. I don't think it's fair that you lied to me.
8. We arrived early just to get good seats.
9. I don't think anyone can solve this problem.
10. That car is more expensive than it ought to be.
11. We had several guests at our house over the holidays.
12. Jan hardly ever enjoys eating vegetables.
13. I was glad when I got the problem off my chest.
14. The quality of meat at that market couldn't be better.
15. Barry called several times but couldn't reach me at home.
16. Pete's a careless person, isn't he?
17. She cleaned her glasses with water in order to see better.
18. He didn't give me the time of day.
19. I understand that the lecturer is a dynamic speaker.
20. It's been quite hot recently, although summer is still two months off.

Answers

1. (C)	2. (A)	3. (D)	4. (B)	5. (B)	6. (C)	7. (A)
8. (B)	9. (B)	10. (D)	11. (C)	12. (A)	13. (C)	14. (A)
15. (D)	16. (B)	17. (B)	18. (C)	19. (A)	20. (C)	

Explanations for Listening Practice A

- In the time between statements (and hopefully during the directions for Part A), you may have been able to preview some of the answer sets. The purpose for doing this is to predict the kind of statement you will hear. Let's look at the important ideas in all of the answer sets.

  Set 1 involves Jane, her diploma, and time.
  Set 2 involves correcting exams.
  Set 3 involves parents and a visit.
  Set 4 MAY involve a man's character.
  Set 5 involves Jim and Mary and a party.
  Set 6 involves a politician and a reporter.
  Set 7 MAY involve someone not telling the truth.
  Set 8 involves seating at some event.
  Set 9 involves the difficulty of a problem.
  Set 10 involves the price of a car.
  Set 11 involves guests and a holiday.
  Set 12 involves vegetables.
  Set 13 MAY involve a special expression using the word *chest*.
  Set 14 involves meat at a store.
  Set 15 involves reaching (contacting) someone.
  Set 16 MAY involve an expression using the word *care*.
  Set 17 MAY involve eyeglasses and clear sight.
  Set 18 MAY involve a special expression using the word *time*.
  Set 19 MAY involve a lecturer.
  Set 20 involves the weather.

- The best sets to preview are those in which some words are used repeatedly. In these sets, the important ideas are more evident. For Listening Practice A, these sets are the ones described above by the words "Set _____ involves..."

- You should not spend much time trying to preview the sets in which the important ideas are not so evident. These are ones described above by the words "Set _____ MAY involve..." The word *may* indicates that it is harder to determine the important ideas. Notice that most of these are in the second half of Part A.

- As you know, most wrong answer choices contain sound-alike words and phrases, words with multiple meanings, and minimal pairs. These forms are intended to confuse you. Let's look at 13:

  SENTENCE YOU HEAR: I was glad when I got the problem off my chest.

  ANSWER CHOICES: (A) I had some problems with my heart.
  (B) I was glad to get a new oak chest.
  (C) When I discussed my problem, I felt better.
  (D) I had problems playing chess.

  The correct answer is (C). The expression *to get a problem off one's chest* is an idiomatic expression. It means "to discuss a situation openly, with the purpose of feeling better." Answer (A) contains the word *heart*, which is associated with the chest area of the body. Answer (B) contains the word *chest*, which here means "a set of drawers." Answer (D) contains the word *chess*, which sounds like *chest*. These are all WRONG answers.

- Notice that wrong answers seem similar to the statement you hear, while the correct answer seems quite different. This fact is true for many of the questions in Part A. A good rule to remember is:

  If you're not sure which answer is correct, choose the one that looks most different from what you hear.

Short Conversations (Part B)

In Part B, you hear a short conversation between two people. Each of these people speaks only once, and the conversation is not repeated. Then you hear a question about what was said. You have 12 seconds to choose the best response to the question.

MODEL

NOTE: M = man
W = woman
Q = question

You will hear: *M:* What a delicious pie! Did you make it?
W: No, I had the bakery do it.
Q: What does the woman mean?

You will read: (A) She asked the man to make it.
(B) The bakery made the pie for her.
(C) She thinks the pie is delicious.
(D) She made it herself.

(A) This answer is incorrect. The woman did not ask the man to make the pie.
(B) This answer is correct. It means the same thing as what the woman said to the man.
(C) This answer is incorrect. The man, not the woman, says that the pie is delicious.
(D) This answer is incorrect. The bakery made it for her.

Types of Conversations

- Most of the conversations in Part B are INFORMAL. The speakers are friends or acquaintances.

  1. You will hear: *W:* Dave, can you help me with this work?
     M: Sure, Pat, if it won't take much time.
     Q: What does the man mean?

  You will read: (A) He has a lot of time to help.
  (B) He needs help with his work.
  (C) He can help her for a while.
  (D) He won't take time to help her.

  Dave indicates that he has only a short time to help Pat, so the correct answer is (C). The informal tone of the conversation suggests that Dave and Pat are probably good friends.

- Because the conversations are generally informal, the language is more IDIOMATIC. Words and phrases with special meaning are used quite often.

  2. You will hear: *M:* This course is a real killer! I'm going to drop out of it.
     W: I may do the same myself.
     Q: What does the man mean?

  You will read: (A) He will drop the woman off at school.
  (B) He enjoys the course very much.
  (C) He dropped his pen on the floor.
  (D) He will stop attending class.

The slang expression *a real killer* means *very difficult*. The idiom *to drop out of* means *to stop attending*. The correct answer is (D).

- Some of the conversations are MORE FORMAL because the speakers have a special relationship, such as doctor/patient, telephone operator/businessman, teacher/student, etc.

  3. You will hear: *M:* Operator, I'd like to place a long-distance collect call.
  　　　　　　　　 W: All lines are busy now, sir. Please hold.
  　　　　　　　　 Q: What does the woman mean?

  　　You will read: (A) The man has to wait for an available line.
  　　　　　　　　 (B) She is very busy making collect calls.
  　　　　　　　　 (C) She will place the long-distance call now.
  　　　　　　　　 (D) She will hold the line open for him.

  The expression *to hold* means *to wait* when it is used for telephone calls. The correct answer is (A). The terms *operator* and *sir* indicate a formal relationship.

Types of Questions

- Some questions ask about DETAILS that are directly mentioned in the conversation. You hear these facts in the conversations and can find them in the answers.

  4. You will hear: *W:* We had fun at the reunion, didn't we?
  　　　　　　　　 M: Yes, it was nice to see old classmates again.
  　　　　　　　　 Q: What do the man and woman mean?

  　　You will read: (A) They are happy to be reunited.
  　　　　　　　　 (B) They enjoyed seeing old friends from their school days.
  　　　　　　　　 (C) Their classmates seemed rather old.
  　　　　　　　　 (D) They didn't have fun at the reunion.

  The terms *fun* and *nice* show enjoyment, and *old classmates* refers to friends from previous school days. These facts indicate that (B) is the correct answer.

- Certain questions are commonly used to ask for details. These questions include the following:
  a. What does the man mean?
  b. What is the woman doing?
  c. What's the man trying to do?
  d. What does the woman want to know?
  e. What is the man asking?

- Question (a.) is a very common one in Part B. The answer to this question will always be a COMPLETE SENTENCE.

  5. You will hear: *W:* Did you feel the earthquake last night?
  　　　　　　　　 M: No, I was sound asleep all night!
  　　　　　　　　 Q: What does the man mean?

  　　You will read: (A) He felt the earthquake.
  　　　　　　　　 (B) The sound of the earthquake woke him up.
  　　　　　　　　 (C) He slept right through the earthquake.
  　　　　　　　　 (D) The earthquake made him feel sleepy.

  All the answers are complete sentences. The expression *sound asleep* shows that the man did not wake up, so the correct answer is (C).

- Answers to questions (b.—e.), however, will probably be INCOMPLETE SENTENCES.

6. You will hear: W: Can you put out the garbage for me?
   M: Just a moment. Let me finish the newspaper.
   Q: What is the man doing?

   You will read: (A) Reading a newspaper.
   (B) Cleaning the house.
   (C) Finishing a newsletter.
   (D) Putting the garbage away.

   The answers are incomplete sentences that begin with participles. As complete sentences, each answer would begin with "He is..." The correct answer is (A).

7. You will hear: M: I found the textbook we need to buy for class.
   W: Great. What did you pay for it?
   Q: What does the woman want to know?

   You will read: (A) When the class starts.
   (B) Where she can buy some glasses.
   (C) Who needs to buy the textbook.
   (D) How much the text costs.

   The answers are incomplete sentences that start with question words. As complete sentences, each answer would begin with "She wants to know..." (D) is correct.

- Some questions require you to make INFERENCES from the conversations. As you have learned, an inference is a conclusion that you must make from the information you are given. The answer is SUGGESTED, not clearly stated as a detail.

8. You will hear: M: Do you feel like going out tonight?
   W: I feel very comfortable in front of the TV.
   Q: What does the woman mean?

   You will read: (A) She wants to go out.
   (B) She wants to go to a comfortable place.
   (C) She doesn't want to leave.
   (D) She wants the man to take the TV out.

   The woman feels comfortable in front of the television, which suggests that she doesn't want to go out. Therefore, (C) is the correct answer.

- Certain questions are commonly used to ask for inferences. These questions include the following:

   a. What does the woman mean?
   b. What can be concluded about the man?
   c. What does the woman imply?
   d. What is the man suggesting?

Notice that question (a.) is used for both detail questions AND inference questions. In either case, the answers are complete sentences.

- Two common types of inference questions involve the LOCATION of a conversation and the IDENTITY of one of the speakers.

9. You will hear: *M:* Have you put the books back on the shelves yet?
   W: No, I have to do some work on the card catalog first.
   Q: Where does this conversation probably take place?

You will read: (A) In a stationery store.
   (B) In a bookstore.
   (C) In a library.
   (D) In a shelving store.

Card catalog and *putting books back on the shelves* suggest that the man and woman are in a library. Therefore, (C) is the correct answer. The question, ''Where does this conversation probably OCCUR?'' could also be used.

10. You will hear: *M:* Is the patient prepared for the operation?
   W: Yes, we're ready to start.
   Q: What is probably the man's occupation?

You will read: (A) A telephone operator.
   (B) A doctor.
   (C) A patient.
   (D) A reading specialist.

Patient and *operation* suggest that the man is a doctor, so (B) is correct. The question, ''What is probably the man's PROFESSION?'' could also be used.

Types of Answer Choices

- The same problem areas mentioned in Part A are true for Part B. Sound-alike words and phrases, words with multiple meanings, and minimal pairs are used in the WRONG answer choices to confuse you.

- The answer choices in Part B are shorter than those in Part A. Some choices are not sentences, but rather PHRASES (parts of sentences). In some cases you can easily predict what the question will be.

11.   (A) Painter.   Possible questions:
        (B) Doctor.
        (C) Bus driver.   What is the woman's occupation?
        (D) Teacher.   What is the man's profession?

12.   (A) In a hospital.   Possible question:
        (B) In a supermarket.
        (C) In a bank.   Where does the conversation
        (D) In a pharmacy.   take place/occur?

13.   (A) Take a walk.   Possible questions:
        (B) Do the dishes.   What's the woman trying to do?
        (C) Go to bed early. What's the man trying to do?
        (D) Work all night.   What will the woman do?

Because the answer choices are shorter than in Part A, it is easier to preview during the instruction period and between questions.

Strategies for Part B

- The strategies suggested in Part A also work in Part B. These points are reviewed below.

  1. Do NOT listen to the directions. Use this time to preview the answer sets. Unlike Part A, it will always be possible for you to preview some answer sets during the directions.
  2. Expect the correct answer to be a PARAPHRASE (restatement) of the details or an INFERENCE (conclusion) suggested by the details.
  3. Expect the correct answer for a paraphrase question to contain SYNONYMS of the words you hear.
  4. Avoid WRONG answer choices containing minimal pairs, sound-alike words and phrases, and words with multiple meanings.
  5. Watch for IDIOMATIC EXPRESSIONS having special meanings.

- Pay careful attention to the details in the very beginning of the conversations. Sometimes a question is difficult because it asks about something the first speaker said.

- If you don't understand a conversation, don't waste time trying to find an answer. Instead, guess at an answer quickly and use the extra time to preview the next answer set. In this way you can get some idea of the kind of question you will hear.

- DO NOT LOOK at the answers while the conversation is being read. Concentrate on the content of the conversation and its connection to the answer choices you have previewed.

Listening Practice B

In the following exercise, you should try to use the strategies you have just learned for Parts A and B. These include:

1. previewing the answers during the directions and between conversations;
2. concentrating on important ideas in each conversation you hear;
3. rephrasing what you hear by using synonyms;
4. watching for idiomatic expressions;
5. being careful to avoid answers containing sound-alike words or phrases, words with multiple meanings, and minimal pairs.

Part B

Directions: In Part B, you hear a short conversation between two people, followed by a question about the conversation. The conversation and question are spoken only one time, so you must listen carefully to understand what is said. After you hear the conversation and question, you will read four possible answers. You must choose the BEST answer to the question you heard. You will then mark the correct answer on your answer sheet.

Look at the following example.

You will hear:

You will read: (A) She believes they had a chance of passing.
                (B) She thinks they studied enough.
                (C) She wishes they could take the test again.
                (D) She thinks it was a bad exam.

The conversation tells you that the woman wishes they had another chance at the exam. The best answer to the question, "What does the woman mean?" is (C), "She wishes they could take the test again." You should mark (C) on your answer sheet.

1. (A) If she has gone skiing before.
   (B) What the weather will be tomorrow.
   (C) When the woman wants to ski.
   (D) Whether the woman has worn a cast before.

2. (A) Professional window cleaner.
   (B) Automotive salesperson.
   (C) Service station attendant.
   (D) Janitorial assistant.

3. (A) She guesses there's a party.
   (B) She has nothing to do at the party.
   (C) She can't go to the party.
   (D) She'll probably go to the party.

GO ON TO THE NEXT PAGE ➤

4. (A) Joe is a serious person.
   (B) Joe is always teasing her.
   (C) She usually knows what Joe means.
   (D) Joe has a serious problem with his leg.

5. (A) In a movie theater.
   (B) In a department store.
   (C) In a fast-food restaurant.
   (D) In a supermarket.

6. (A) He got on at the wrong bus stop.
   (B) He took the wrong bus.
   (C) He was all wound up.
   (D) He went in the right direction.

7. (A) She has never seen a strange movie before.
   (B) She agrees with the man.
   (C) She thinks it's a strange movie theater.
   (D) She's sure that the movie is good.

8. (A) He is working on the grant with Joan.
   (B) He already works for the government.
   (C) He told Joan about the government grant.
   (D) He already knows about Joan's new grant.

9. (A) Have her daughter counseled by a psychologist.
   (B) Counsel her daughter herself.
   (C) Discipline her daughter more seriously.
   (D) Put her daughter on a council.

10. (A) He doesn't have a job.
    (B) He can't associate with his boss well.
    (C) His boss sent him out on a job.
    (D) Bob's having problems hearing his boss.

11. (A) He should go to class.
    (B) She wants to miss class too.
    (C) She wishes she were in his position.
    (D) She wants him to skip class.

12. (A) On Monday and Wednesday morning.
    (B) On Tuesday and Thursday morning.
    (C) Three times that week.
    (D) On Monday and Wednesday afternoon.

13. (A) She helped to write Tom's thesis.
    (B) Tom typed and proofread her thesis.
    (C) She is very familiar with Tom's thesis.
    (D) She's sure that Tom didn't finish his thesis.

14. (A) Attend a lecture.
    (B) Look after her professor.
    (C) Take care of her child.
    (D) See Professor Nye.

15. (A) She lends her car only to close friends.
    (B) She is hesitant to borrow his car.
    (C) Her friends hesitate to lend her a car.
    (D) She is reluctant to lend her car to anyone.

STOP STOP STOP STOP STOP STOP STOP

Transcript and Answers begin on the following page.

Transcript and Answers for Listening Practice B

Example

M: Too bad we both failed the exam. I guess we didn't study hard enough for it.
W: If only we had another chance at it.
Q: What does the woman mean?

1. *W:* Will you go skiing tomorrow?
   M: Probably. Do you know the forecast?
   Q: What does the man want to know?

2. *W:* Please check the oil and water as well as the tires.
   M: Of course. Would you like your windows cleaned, too?
   Q: What is probably the man's occupation?

3. *M:* Going to the party?
   W: I guess so.
   Q: What does the woman mean?

4. *M:* I never know whether Joe is serious or not.
   W: I know what you mean. He's always pulling my leg, too!
   Q: What does the woman mean?

5. *W:* Excuse me. Could you help me locate the canned fruit?
   M: Certainly. You'll find them past the dairy section, in aisle 3.
   Q: Where does this conversation take place?

6. *M:* Sorry I'm late. I caught the wrong bus and wound up going in the opposite direction.
   W: Next time pay more attention to where you're going.
   Q: Why is the man late?

7. *M:* This is one of the strangest movies I've ever seen.
   W: It sure is.
   Q: What does the woman mean?

8. *W:* Have you heard? Joan got a great grant from the government.
   M: So I've been told.
   Q: What does the man mean?

9. *W:* My daughter is having some discipline problems at school.
   M: You should have a psychologist counsel her.
   Q: What should the woman do?

10. *M:* I hear Bob's having difficulty getting along with his boss.
    W: Yes, I wouldn't be surprised if he's out of a job soon.
    Q: What is Bob's problem?

11. *M:* I feel like skipping class today.
    W: I wouldn't if I were you.
    Q: What is the woman suggesting?

12. *M1:* I'd like to reserve this room on Monday and Wednesday from 9 to 11 A.M.
    M2: I'm sorry. It's only available in the afternoon on those days, but you can use it Tuesday and Thursday mornings if you'd like.
    Q: When does the man need the room?

13. *M:* Did you know that Tom finally finished his thesis?
    W: I sure do! I proofread it all for him!!
    Q: What does the woman mean?

14. *W:* Yesterday I had to look after my sick one all day.
    M: So that's why I didn't see you at Professor Nye's lecture.
    Q: What did the woman have to do?

15. *M:* Could you possibly lend me your car?
    W: Well, I'm usually hesitant to do that, even with friends.
    Q: What is the woman implying?

Answers   1. (B)   2. (C)   3. (D)   4. (B)   5. (D)   6. (B)
            7. (B)   8. (D)   9. (A)   10. (B)   11. (A)   12. (A)
           13. (C)   14. (C)   15. (D)

Explanations for Listening Practice B

• During the period of directions for Part B, you should have had time to preview several sets of answer choices. Some answer sets contain short phrases, so you can more easily guess what the questions will be about. Let's look at these:

   Set 1 involves KNOWING something.
   Set 2 involves IDENTITY.
   Set 5 involves PLACE.
   Set 9 involves DOING something (ACTION).
   Set 12 involves TIME.
   Set 14 involves DOING something (ACTION).

• The other answer sets contain complete sentences and thus take more effort to preview.

   Set 3 involves a party.
   Set 4 involves something about a man named Joe.
   Set 6 involves taking the bus.
   Set 7 involves a movie.
   Set 8 involves a grant.
   Set 10 involves a man's job.
   Set 11 involves going to class.
   Set 13 involves Tom's thesis.
   Set 15 involves lending a car.

• Some students prefer to preview a consecutive series of answer sets (for example, 1–6). Others prefer concentrating on the sets containing phrases, which are generally easier to preview. It is impossible to say which is better; the choice is yours.

Academic Talks and Long Conversations (Part C)

In Part C, you will hear academic talks and conversations that are longer than those in Part B. In a talk, one person is providing information on a topic; in a conversation, two people are discussing a situation together. After each talk or conversation, there are several questions about what you just heard. You have 12 seconds to answer each question.

Part C is quite difficult becaues you are NOT allowed to take any written notes while you listen. You are expected to memorize the important information.

<u>MODEL</u>

You will hear: Our lesson today is on shifts in population between urban and suburban areas. Until recently, the middle and upper classes were moving out of urban areas in record numbers, leaving the inner city to the poor. Affluent citizens chose the comfort and safety of the suburbs over the crime of downtown. This trend is slowly changing, however, as city governments make an effort to revitalize downtown areas and attract the affluent back.

You will hear: 1. Who mainly lives in the inner city now?

You will read: (A) The upper class.
                 (B) City government.
                 (C) The poverty striken.
                 (D) The middle class.

This talk is given by a professor to his class. It is the introductory part of a longer lecture. The correct answer is (C), because the poor (the poverty stricken) live in the inner city.

NOTE: Only one question is given in this model. However, on the real exam, there will be several questions for each talk or conversation.

Types of Talks and Conversations

Almost any kind of talk or conversation could occur in Part C, but certain types are more likely. These are explained below.

- LONG CONVERSATION—Two speakers have an extended conversation (called a *dialogue*). The topic of this conversation is usually related to school. The first thing you hear in Part C is often a conversation.

  1. You will hear: *M:* Hi, Sue, how's it going?
                       W: Oh, hi, Frank. Just fine. How are your classes?
                       M: Pretty good. I'm glad this is my last semester here, though.
                       W: Why is that? I thought you were enjoying school.
                       M: I was, but now I'm getting tired of it. I'm ready for the real world.
                       W: What are you planning to do when you graduate?
                       M: First I want to travel a little, and then get a good job as a computer specialist.
                       W: Sounds good. I still have three semesters to go until I'm done.
                       M: You'll make it! Well, see you later.
                       W: Bye.

The conversation is school-related. In this case, it is between two students who know each other. Other dialogues might involve a student talking to a teacher, a librarian, an admissions advisor, a lab assistant, etc. The conversation is generally informal.

- ACADEMIC LECTURE—A professor or visiting expert gives a short lecture to a class. The lecture is on a topic related to the subject of the course.

2. You will hear: I'm very glad that Professor Peters has given me the chance to talk to you today on the risks involved in using computers in business. As a computer behavior consultant, I see people every day who cause serious problems in their company as a result of their attitudes towards computers. There are the "gamers," people who spend working time playing computer games behind the boss's back. There are the "techies," those who get so wrapped up in learning the technology that they become less productive. Yet others are "empire builders," those who try to gain control and power with their computer expertise. Finally, there are the "computer-phobes," those who are so afraid of computers that they will have nothing to do with the machines or the people who work with them.

The speaker is a visiting expert who is talking to a class of business students. The talk is the introductory part of a longer lecture.

- ORIENTATION SESSION—Someone gives information on a part of a college or university to a group of students. The orientation might be on health services, the library, computer facilities, the student center, etc.

3. You will hear: I'd like to welcome you to the Arts and Crafts Center on campus. As new art majors, you will undoubtedly have many opportunities to use our fine facilities. The purpose of this orientation is to inform you of the different services we offer and of the rules we expect all students to follow. Before we begin the orientation, let me remind you that only students with valid ID cards will be allowed to use the Center. Please do not try to gain entrance without proving that you are a current student. Any questions about that? OK, let's begin.

The speaker is probably a staff member of the Arts and Crafts Center. The talk is the beginning of an orientation for new art majors.

Types of Questions

A wide variety of questions can appear in Part C, but certain types tend to occur regularly. These are listed below.

- The following questions might be used for ANY talk or conversation:

  Who is the speaker? *or* Who are the speakers?
  Where does the conversation/talk take place?
  When does the conversation/talk take place?

- For a CONVERSATION, further questions might be:

  What are the man and woman discussing?
  What is the man/woman going to do next week/month/year?
  What does the man/woman want to know?

- For a TALK, further questions might be:

  What is the main topic of the lecture?
  What is the speaker's field of work?
  Who is the speaker lecturing to? *or* Who is in the audience?

- Again, many other questions are possible. In most cases, they will ask about DETAILS in the talk or conversation. Few questions require you to make an inference from what was said.

Types of Answer Choices

The answer choices in Part C are much shorter than those in Parts A or B. For this reason, it is easier to preview the answer sets and to predict what questions will be asked.

- Some answer sets involve the IDENTITY of the speaker or speakers.

  4. (A) A scientist.
     (B) A visiting scholar.
     (C) A conservation expert.
     (D) A physicist.

  The question for this answer set will ask the identity of a single person, probably the one giving a talk or lecture.

  5. (A) Two students.
     (B) A student and a professor.
     (C) Two professors.
     (D) A psychologist and a librarian.

  The question for this answer set will ask for the identity of two persons having a conversation.

- Some answer sets involve the TIME of the talk or conversation.

  6. (A) In the morning.
     (B) At midday.
     (C) In the early afternoon.
     (D) In the late evening.

  The question for this answer set may seem very obvious. However, the talk or conversation may include references to different times of the day, which makes choosing the correct answer more difficult.

- Some answer sets involve the LOCATION of a talk or conversation.

  7. (A) In the bookstore.
     (B) In front of the library.
     (C) Near the cafeteria.
     (D) By the parking lot.

  Again, the question may seem obvious, but the talk or conversation will probably mention more than one location, only one of which is appropriate as an answer to the question.

- Most of the answer choices in Part C, like those above, are phrases. Occasionally, however, sentence forms occur. You should preview these in the same way you preview the answers in Parts A and B.

    8. (A) He forgot to leave her a message.
       (B) He put the note in the wrong place.
       (C) The note was addressed to the wrong person.
       (D) She didn't notice the paper on the dresser.

    You could expect the question to be about a note and where it was put.

Strategies for Part C

- During the directions, preview as many answer sets as possible. The answer choices tend to be quite short, so you should be able to preview most of the sets.

- As you do so, make mental notes on the probable topics and the types of questions to expect. As we have discussed, you should see some sets that are about identity, time, and location.

- Once the talk or conversation starts, it is much better to listen carefully WITHOUT looking at the answers. This allows you to concentrate on the main ideas and important details.

- However, in reality, many students feel they have to look at the answers, especially with long talks. Sometimes this works well because the order of questions is usually the same as the order in which the information is presented on the tape.

- If you feel you must look at the answers while listening, do the following:

    a. During the directions, preview some answer sets carefully to predict the details you must listen for.
    b. Concentrate on recognizing these details in what you hear. When you think you recognize an answer, make a mental note of the correct letter choice.
    c. Mark your answer on the answer sheet AFTER you have heard each question.

Listening Practice C

In the following exercise, you should try to use the strategies you have just learned for Part C. These include:

1. previewing the answer choices during the instruction period and between questions;
2. listening carefully without looking at the answers;
3. concentrating on the important ideas in each talk or conversation.

Part C

Directions: In Part C, you will hear some talks and conversations. Each talk or conversation is followed by some questions. The conversations or talks and the questions about them are spoken only one time, so you must listen carefully. After you hear each question, you will read four possible answers. You must choose the BEST answer to the question. You will then mark the correct answer on your answer sheet.

Listen to this sample talk.

You will hear:

Now look at the following example.

You will hear:

You will read: (A) A new student.
(B) A university professor.
(C) The head of the Counseling Center.
(D) A department secretary.

The question, "Who is the speaker?" is best answered by (C), "The head of the Counseling Center." This is the answer you should choose.

Now look at the next example.

You will hear:

You will read: (A) To welcome new students to the university.
(B) To change the counseling services.
(C) To take advantage of the students.
(D) To inform new students of counseling services.

The question "What is the speaker's main responsibility?" is best answered by (D), "To inform new students of counseling services." This is the answer you should choose.

GO ON TO THE NEXT PAGE ➤

1. (A) A married couple.
   (B) University students.
   (C) Office secretaries.
   (D) Air conditioning technicians.

2. (A) In a professor's office.
   (B) In the library.
   (C) In a classroom.
   (D) In a student lounge.

3. (A) He is a sophomore at the university.
   (B) He is a graduate student.
   (C) He is Sue's boyfriend.
   (D) He is in his first term at the university.

4. (A) The professor is a good one.
   (B) The professor is having some coffee with a friend.
   (C) The professor may never arrive at class.
   (D) The professor may let them go in 15 minutes.

5. (A) A university librarian.
   (B) Data control supervisor.
   (C) A professor in the business department.
   (D) Operations manager of the computer center.

6. (A) Giving an orientation session.
   (B) Lecturing to a class.
   (C) Introducing new students to each other.
   (D) Advising students on business classes.

7. (A) Operations personnel.
   (B) Business majors.
   (C) Graduate students.
   (D) Student assistants.

8. (A) One.
   (B) Two.
   (C) Three.
   (D) Four.

9. (A) Near the business building.
   (B) At the end of the hall.
   (C) Opposite the computer laboratory.
   (D) Across from the restrooms.

10. (A) He prepares the computer printouts.
    (B) He operates the computers for students.
    (C) He opens student accounts.
    (D) He assists students with their work.

11. (A) In the library.
    (B) In the administration building.
    (C) Near the cashier's office.
    (D) Across from the student center.

12. (A) In the early morning.
    (B) In the middle of the day.
    (C) In the late afternoon.
    (D) In the evening.

13. (A) A meal card for the cafeteria.
    (B) A sticker for her bicycle.
    (C) A college catalog and class schedule.
    (D) A parking permit.

14. (A) He rides a motorcycle.
    (B) He drives a car.
    (C) He rides a bicycle.
    (D) He takes the bus.

15. (A) She's glad it is reasonable.
    (B) She's delighted it is rather inexpensive.
    (C) She's amazed it is so costly.
    (D) She's shocked she can't afford one yet.

Transcript and Answers for Listening Practice C

Example

I'd like to welcome you to the Counseling Center. As head of the department, I am responsible for informing you, as new students, of the ways we can provide assistance. Many students do not take advantage of our academic and personal counseling services, but we are working to change that situation.

Example 1 Who is the speaker?
Example 2 What is the speaker's responsibility?

Questions 1–4 refer to the following conversation.

W: Hi. My name's Sue.
M: Hi. I'm Alex. It's hot in here, isn't it?
W: It certainly is. I hope it isn't like this all semester.
M: It might be! They have problems with the cooling system all the time.
W: So you went here last year?
M: Yeah, I'm a sophomore this year. How about you?
W: This is my first term. I don't know anybody here.
M: Well, you do now! How about having some coffee after this class?
W: Sounds good, but we may get to go sooner than we think. The professor's already 15 minutes late!

1. Who are the speakers?
2. Where does this conversation take place?
3. What do we learn about Alex?
4. What does Sue suggest about the professor?

Questions 5–10 refer to the following talk.

Good afternoon. I'm Vera Simpson, operations manager of the Campus Computer Center. As entering business majors, I'm sure that you will be spending as much time here as you will in the library. Before I begin the orientation, I'd like to introduce you to a couple of individuals you will deal with frequently. Standing on my left is Jane Carson, supervisor of Data Control. You will see her when you need to open an account and to pick up your computer printouts. You may already know that Data Control is up the hall across from the computer laboratory. On my right is Jeff Burdick, student assistant for the laboratory. Since he is a graduate student in business, he will be able to help you not only with the operation of the computers but with problems you might have with your assignments as well.

5. Who is Vera Simpson?
6. What is Simpson doing?
7. Who is in the audience?
8. How many people are standing with Simpson?
9. Where is Data Control located?
10. What is Jeff Burdick's role?

Questions 11–15 refer to the following conversation.

W: Excuse me. This is my first day on campus! Could you tell me where the financial aid office is?
M: Sure. Do you see that tall building? That's the library. As soon as you pass it, you'll see the administration building on the left.

W: Is financial aid in that building?

M: Yes, it is. You have to take the elevator to the second floor, then go to the end of the hall. You'd better hurry, though, because it's almost five o'clock.

W: Oh, OK. Could you also tell me where I can get a parking sticker for my car?

M: You can buy that at the cashier's office. It's in the one-story building next to the student center, about 50 feet past the cafeteria.

W: Oh, I know where that is. Do you know how much a sticker costs?

M: I have a motorcycle, so I'm not sure, but I think it's $80 a semester.

W: Wow, that's not cheap! Well, I guess I have no choice. Thanks for your help.

M: Anytime.

11. Where is the financial aid office located?
12. When does the conversation take place?
13. What does the woman want to buy?
14. How does the man get to school?
15. What is the woman's reaction to the cost of a sticker?

Answers   1. (B)   2. (C)   3. (A)   4. (C)   5. (D)   6. (A)

              7. (B)   8. (B)   9. (C)   10. (D)   11. (B)   12. (C)

            13. (D)   14. (A)   15. (C)

Explanations for Listening Practice C

- The first thing you listen to is a typical conversation between two students. You are asked questions about:

  1. the identity of the speakers;
  2. the location of the conversation;
  3. something that is true about the man; and
  4. something that is true about the professor.

- The second item is a typical orientation to the computer center for new business majors. You are asked questions about:

  5. the identity of the speaker;
  6. the activity of the speaker;
  7. the identity of the audience;
  8. the quantity of something;
  9. the location of something; and
  10. the activity of some man.

- The third item is another conversation between two students. You are asked questions about:

  11. the location of some place on campus;
  12. the time of the conversation;
  13. some item that is being discussed;
  14. the man's means of transportation; and
  15. what the woman thinks about the cost of something.

- As with Parts A and B, the key to doing well in Part C is the ability to determine the factors above when you preview the answers. Remember that there are two times when you can preview:

  a. during the time when instructions are given;
  b. during the one to four seconds after you answer a question and before you hear the next question.

If you can learn to do this well on all three parts of the Listening Comprehension section, you can greatly increase your chances of getting a good score.

Listening Practice Test

SECTION 1
LISTENING COMPREHENSION

This section tests your understanding of spoken English. It is divided into three parts.

Part A

<u>Directions:</u> In Part A, you will hear a short statement. This statement is spoken just once. It is not written for you, so you must listen carefully to understand its meaning.

After you hear the statement, you will read four possible answers. You must choose the answer that is CLOSEST IN MEANING to the statement you hear. You will then mark the correct answer on your answer sheet.

    Example I

       You will hear:

       You will read: (A) Tom's friend was all right.
                     (B) Tom and his friend had a long argument.
                     (C) Tom glued the end to the light.
                     (D) Tom spent the night alone.

You heard, "Tom argued with his friend all night." Sentence (B), "Tom and his friend had a long argument," has the closest meaning. You should mark (B) on your answer sheet.

    Example II

       You will hear:

       You will read: (A) Can you help me review the exam?
                     (B) What time is the test?
                     (C) I don't have time to bring the test.
                     (D) Can I go to the test right now?

You heard, "Do you have time to go over the test with me?" Sentence (A), "Can you help me review the exam?" has the closest meaning. You should mark (A) on your answer sheet.

GO ON TO THE NEXT PAGE

1. (A) I'm still bothered by it.
   (B) My brother continues to look a lot like me.
   (C) I bought a lot of things at the store.
   (D) I'm not annoyed anymore.

2. (A) He got the last pair of tickets to the concert.
   (B) He didn't know he had to have tickets.
   (C) He lost his keys and forgot the tickets as well.
   (D) He got the tickets after he found his keys.

3. (A) How is it outside today?
   (B) Today isn't very nice.
   (C) There's ice on the sidewalk.
   (D) The weather is quite nice.

4. (A) This is a movie for the whole family.
   (B) Are you familiar with this movie?
   (C) It doesn't seem like a good movie.
   (D) I think I've seen this movie before.

5. (A) President Jones met with us for some time.
   (B) We neglected to meet with President Jones at the conference.
   (C) President Jones forgot to reserve time to meet with us.
   (D) President Jones neglected to set the time for the conference.

6. (A) Is your coat with your hat?
   (B) Does this coat and hat belong to you?
   (C) Where did you put your coat and hat?
   (D) Does this hat look good with this coat?

7. (A) It's all right if you come.
   (B) They want you to come with me.
   (C) If you feel fine, you can come.
   (D) You can come if you can find us.

8. (A) Did you win this sweater as a prize?
   (B) I think they put the wrong price on this sweater.
   (C) Take this sweater over to the cashier.
   (D) Isn't this sweater too expensive?

9. (A) Sue forgot that she had an exam to prepare for.
   (B) Sue wrote a note to her friend during the exam.
   (C) She prepared her notes before the exam.
   (D) Sue doesn't have notes to prepare for the exam.

10. (A) Mike lay in a daze on the bed.
    (B) Mike had to stay in bed for almost a week.
    (C) It took several days for Mike to buy a bed.
    (D) Mike's bed lay on the floor.

11. (A) What difference does it make?
    (B) I'd like to know what the difference is.
    (C) He and I are quite different.
    (D) I don't care what he said.

12. (A) He wanted an older car.
    (B) The old car did not suit his needs.
    (C) He used the car until it became too old.
    (D) What kind of used car did he want?

GO ON TO THE NEXT PAGE ▶

13. (A) Their relatives are too weak to show up.
    (B) Next week their relatives will come.
    (C) Their relatives will arrive in two weeks.
    (D) They showed me where their relatives live.

14. (A) I can't believe what he told me.
    (B) He told me that he did it first.
    (C) He didn't believe that I told him first.
    (D) He didn't inform me before he did it.

15. (A) Mr. Peters was tired of being supervisor.
    (B) Mr. Peters served as manager's assistant until last month.
    (C) As of last month, Mr. Peters is no longer manager.
    (D) Mr. Peters became regional manager a month ago.

16. (A) Seldom does Bertha miss morning class.
    (B) It is unusual for Bertha to go to morning classes.
    (C) Bertha tends to like classes before noon.
    (D) Bertha sells tennis lessons for a living.

17. (A) I suspect it was done deliberately.
    (B) I'm convinced that the accident never happened.
    (C) The accident claimed several lives.
    (D) They filed an insurance claim for the accident.

18. (A) Bill had no excuse for leaving.
    (B) Bill is very good at making excuses.
    (C) Bill excused Pat from the meeting.
    (D) They gave no excuse for leaving Bill alone.

19. (A) The university should have better professors.
    (B) He's one of the top professors at the university.
    (C) The university has an excellent faculty.
    (D) Some professors are not as good as others.

20. (A) It can't be altered at this point.
    (B) We should change it before he finds out.
    (C) We can't leave it the way it is.
    (D) He should approve the changes before he leaves.

GO ON TO THE NEXT PAGE

Part B

Directions: In Part B, you hear a short conversation between two people, followed by a question about the conversation. The conversation and question are spoken only one time, so you must listen carefully to understand what is said. After you hear the conversation and question, you will read four possible answers. You must choose the BEST answer to the question you heard. You will then mark the correct answer on your answer sheet.

Look at the following example.

You will hear:

You will read: (A) She believes they had a chance of passing.
(B) She thinks they studied enough.
(C) She wishes they could take the test again.
(D) She thinks it was a bad exam.

The conversation tells you that the woman wishes they had another chance at the exam. The best answer to the question, "What does the woman mean?" is (C), "She wishes they could take the test again." You should mark (C) on your answer sheet.

21. (A) He's going to run for gas.
(B) They need gas for the car soon.
(C) He sees a gas station ahead.
(D) They won't be able to find gas.

22. (A) In a drugstore.
(B) In a post office.
(C) In a hospital.
(D) In a supermarket.

23. (A) He didn't have any ideas to express.
(B) He spoke enough at the meeting.
(C) He couldn't think that morning.
(D) He should have spoken up more.

24. (A) She is very active.
(B) She is usually pale.
(C) She is somewhat sick.
(D) She has to save energy.

25. (A) She wants to have a picnic outside.
(B) She hopes to eat in the car.
(C) She wants to park the car.
(D) She thinks it's a nice park.

26. (A) He's not sure where it is.
(B) Sam borrowed the hammer.
(C) He can't lend the hammer.
(D) The hammer belongs to John.

27. (A) The food isn't fresh.
(B) She wants to know whether vegetables are sold or not.
(C) The store doesn't sell vegetables.
(D) She agrees with the man.

GO ON TO THE NEXT PAGE

28. (A) He paid more for the suit than he admitted.
    (B) He doesn't want to reveal the price of the suit.
    (C) He cares for the suit more than the woman does.
    (D) The suit was admitted as evidence.

29. (A) It's a rough one.
    (B) It's one she likes.
    (C) It's far from where she lives.
    (D) It doesn't require any homework.

30. (A) Make a purchase in a supermarket.
    (B) Obtain help from customer service.
    (C) Order some food in a restaurant.
    (D) Wait patiently for some assistance.

31. (A) The man doesn't need to check the battery.
    (B) The tow truck will come soon.
    (C) He can get a battery from the tow truck driver.
    (D) There might be a problem with the electrical system.

32. (A) It's not his fault.
    (B) He was afraid it was going to be bad.
    (C) He wants to go there again.
    (D) He wanted to waste some time.

33. (A) James has decided to keep the tape recorder.
    (B) James has to be constantly reminded.
    (C) She will return the tape recorder to James.
    (D) James is about to return the tape recorder.

34. (A) He didn't have any reasons for quitting his work.
    (B) He quit for the wrong reasons.
    (C) He hasn't shared his reasons for giving up his job.
    (D) He's given different reasons to various friends.

35. (A) Postpone finding a tenant until he feels better.
    (B) Rent an apartment himself.
    (C) Look for someone to rent his apartment.
    (D) Get on the roof to fix the antenna.

GO ON TO THE NEXT PAGE

Part C

Directions: In Part C, you will hear some talks and conversations. Each talk or conversation is followed by some questions. The conversations or talks and the questions about them are spoken only one time, so you must listen carefully. After you hear each question, you will read four possible answers. You must choose the BEST answer to the question. You will then mark the correct answer on your answer sheet.

Listen to this sample talk.

You will hear:

Now look at the following example.

You will hear:

You will read: (A) A new student.
(B) A university professor.
(C) The head of the Counseling Center.
(D) A department secretary.

The question "Who is the speaker?" is best answered by (C), "The head of the Counseling Center." This is the answer you should choose.

Now look at the next example.

You will hear:

You will read: (A) To welcome new students to the university.
(B) To change the counseling services.
(C) To take advantage of the students.
(D) To inform new students of counseling services.

The question "What is the speaker's main responsibility?" is best answered by (D), "To inform new students of counseling services." This is the answer you should choose.

36. (A) Two students.
(B) A professor and a student.
(C) An administrator and a secretary.
(D) A department clerk and a student.

37. (A) In a graduate admissions office.
(B) In a student housing office.
(C) In an undergraduate admissions office.
(D) In a university counseling center.

GO ON TO THE NEXT PAGE ➤

38. (A) A registration form for the spring term.
    (B) A catalog for undergraduate studies.
    (C) An application for the fall term.
    (D) Admission to the graduate division.

39. (A) Close the fall term to new applications.
    (B) Accept new applications for the spring term.
    (C) Refuse twice as many students as usual.
    (D) Stop accepting new employment applications.

40. (A) Do some research at the county library.
    (B) Wait until next term to apply again.
    (C) Pick up a catalog at the county library.
    (D) Apply to another school.

41. (A) A driving instructor.
    (B) A university administrator.
    (C) A clerical worker.
    (D) A business executive.

42. (A) Truck drivers.
    (B) University employees.
    (C) Insurance agents.
    (D) College students.

43. (A) To become better workers.
    (B) To learn how to drive defensively.
    (C) To receive orientation for new employees.
    (D) To learn how to repair university vehicles.

44. (A) The afternoon.
    (B) Midday.
    (C) The morning.
    (D) The evening.

45. (A) Once a month.
    (B) Once a year.
    (C) Twice a year.
    (D) Once every five years.

46. (A) He didn't have a parking permit.
    (B) He had been speeding.
    (C) The parking meter had expired.
    (D) He was in the store too long.

47. (A) An old ticket.
    (B) A note of explanation.
    (C) A protective cover.
    (D) Some money for the meter.

48. (A) Be more careful next time.
    (B) Cite him for the parking violation.
    (C) Cancel the ticket.
    (D) Accept his payment immediately.

49. (A) He has other errands to do.
    (B) He has to get back to work soon.
    (C) His family is waiting for him at home.
    (D) He doesn't want to get into trouble.

50. (A) Buying a quick lunch.
    (B) Accompanying a friend to class.
    (C) Picking up concert tickets.
    (D) Getting something on campus.

Transcript and Answers for Listening Practice Test

Part A

Example I Tom argued with his friend all night.
Example II Do you have time to go over the test with me?

1. It continues to bother me a lot.
2. Not only did he lose his keys, but he also forgot the tickets.
3. How nice it is outside today!
4. This movie *does* seem familiar.
5. President Jones neglected to set aside time to confer with us.
6. Are these your coat and hat?
7. If you want to come, it's fine with us.
8. This sweater is overpriced, don't you think?
9. Sue wishes she had taken notes to prepare for the exam.
10. Mike was laid up in bed for several days.
11. Whatever he says makes no difference to me.
12. The used car was older than what he wanted.
13. Their relatives will show up the week after next.
14. I can't believe that he did it without telling me first.
15. Mr. Peters served as manager until he retired last month.
16. Bertha seldom attends classes in the morning.
17. They claim it was an accident, but I'm not convinced.
18. Leave it to Bill to come up with an excuse like that!
19. The professors at that university are topnotch, I'll bet.
20. It's too late to change it, so leave it the way it is.

Answers	1. (A)	2. (C)	3. (D)	4. (D)	5. (C)	6. (B)
	7. (A)	8. (D)	9. (D)	10. (B)	11. (D)	12. (B)
	13. (C)	14. (D)	15. (C)	16. (B)	17. (A)	18. (B)
	19. (C)	20. (A)				

Part B

Example

M: Too bad we both failed the exam. I guess we didn't study hard enough for it.
W: If only we had another chance at it.
Q: What does the woman mean?

21. *W:* I don't see a gas station anywhere ahead.
    M: I hope we find one before we run out of gas.
    Q: What does the man mean?

22. *M:* Could you tell me where the X-ray department is?
    W: Go down the hall and turn left at the pharmacy. It's just past the nurse's clinic.
    Q: Where does this conversation take place?

23. *W:* You didn't speak up at the meeting today.
    M: I couldn't think of anything to say.
    Q: What does the man mean?

24. *M:* You look a bit pale today.
    W: I know. I just don't seem to have much energy.
    Q: What can be concluded about the woman?

25. *M:* Do you think it will be nice at the park?
    W: I hope so. I'd hate to eat in the car!
    Q: What does the woman mean?

26. *M1:* Could you lend me this hammer, John?
    M2: I'd like to, but it belongs to Sam.
    Q: What does John imply about the hammer?

27. *M:* The vegetables sold here look very fresh.
    W: Don't they!
    Q: What do we learn from the woman's response?

28. *W:* How much did you pay for that suit?
    M: More than I care to admit!
    Q: What does the man mean?

29. *M:* Are you enjoying the seminar you're taking?
    W: So far I am, even though the homework's a bit rough.
    Q: How does the woman feel about the seminar?

30. *W:* Waiter! Could we have some service, please?
    M: I'll be with you in a moment, ma'am.
    Q: What is the woman trying to do?

31. *M:* My car won't start. I'd better call a tow truck.
    W: Shouldn't you check the battery first?
    Q: What is the woman suggesting?

32. *W:* What a waste of time! I'll never go there again.
    M: I had no way of knowing it would be so bad.
    Q: What does the man mean?

33. *M:* James still hasn't returned my tape recorder.
    W: You just have to keep after him about it.
    Q: What does the woman mean?

34. *M1:* Why did Tom quit his job?
    M2: I have no idea! He hasn't told anyone his reasons.
    Q: What are the men saying about Tom?

35. *W:* Have you already found a tenant for your apartment?
    M: I haven't started looking yet, but I'd better get on it.
    Q: What is the man going to do?

Answers   21. (B)   22. (C)   23. (A)   24. (C)   25. (A)   26. (C)
            27. (D)   28. (B)   29. (B)   30. (C)   31. (D)   32. (A)
            33. (B)   34. (C)   35. (C)

Part C

Example

I'd like to welcome you to the Counseling Center. As head of the department, I am responsible for informing you, as new students, of the ways we can provide assistance. Many students do not take advantage of our academic and personal counseling services, but we are working to change that situation.

Example 1 Who is the speaker?
Example 2 What is the speaker's main responsibility?

Questions 36–40 refer to the following conversation.

W: Next, please.

M: Hi. I'd like an application for admission to the fall semester.

W: I'm sorry, but the application period for that term closed a week ago.

M: I don't believe it! It's only the first of the year!

W: I know, but the university has already received twice as many applications as last year, so the administration has decided to stop accepting new ones.

M: Well, what can I do now?

W: You could file an application for the spring term of next year.

M: I can't wait that long. I've already made arrangements for an apartment locally.

W: Then I recommend you try one of the two-year community colleges. Their registration deadlines are usually after ours.

M: That might work. Do you know where I can pick up a class schedule?

W: Most county libraries are stocked with copies. Good luck!

36. Who are the speakers?
37. Where does this conversation probably take place?
38. What does the man want?
39. What did the university administration recently decide to do?
40. What is the man going to do?

Questions 41–45 refer to the following talk.

Good morning. I'm Tom Jackson of the Better Driving Institute. Most of you are here because you expect to drive on official business for the university this coming year. As you know, the university's insurance coverage requires that employees take a defensive driving seminar once a year to remain qualified to operate university vehicles. This rule applies to every employee, from the top administrator to the average clerical worker.

The information you learn here will be useful not only when you are at work, but whenever you are behind the wheel. In some cases, insurance companies will give you a discount on your premium for completing this course. We'll work for about an hour, take a short break, and then work another hour until lunchtime. We'll only be together for a brief period, but I'll try to make it worthwhile. At least you're here instead of working! All right, let's get started.

41. Who is the speaker?
42. Who is in the audience?
43. Why is the audience taking the course?
44. What time of day is it?
45. How often is it necessary to take the course?

Questions 46–50 refer to the following conversation.

M: Excuse me. Did you just give me this ticket?

W: Yes, I did, sir. Your parking meter has expired.

M: But I put a note on the windshield explaining that I would be right back!

W: I read it, but I still have to write out a ticket for the violation.

M: Oh, come on! I'm a visitor on campus, and I was in the bookstore for less than ten minutes.

W: It wouldn't matter if you were gone for only 30 seconds, sir. You broke the law and I have to cite you.

M: Couldn't you please void the ticket for me? I won't let it happen again.

W: I could get into a lot of trouble for doing that. The law's the law.

M: How much is the ticket?

W: I believe it's $15.

M: Well, that's not too bad. Please hurry up so that I can finish my other errands before going home.

W: I'm going as fast as I can, sir. You'll just have to be patient.

46. Why did the man receive a ticket?
47. What did the man leave on his car?
48. What does the man want the policewoman to do about the ticket?
49. Why is the man impatient?
50. What was the man probably doing while away from his car?

Answers 36. (D)   37. (C)   38. (C)   39. (A)   40. (D)   41. (A)
42. (B)   43. (B)   44. (C)   45. (B)   46. (C)   47. (B)
48. (C)   49. (A)   50. (D)

STRUCTURE AND WRITTEN EXPRESSION

The second section of the TOEFL exam tests your knowledge of English grammar and usage. Both the short-form and the long-form versions (described in the Preface) are composed of two parts:

Structure (Part A)
Written Expression (Part B)

For the short-form TOEFL, you have 25 minutes to complete the 40 questions in Section 2. You should spend 10 minutes on Part A and 15 minutes on Part B.

For the long-form TOEFL, you have 35 minutes to complete the 60 questions in Section 2. You should spend 15 minutes on Part A and 20 minutes on Part B.

NOTE: On the TOEFL exam, only Section 1 is formally divided into three parts (Part A, Part B, and Part C). For some reason, the two parts of Section 2 are not identified in this way. In this handbook, we will use ''A'' and ''B'' as a convenient way to refer to each part.

Structure (Part A)

In Part A you will read sentences that are incomplete in some way. You will choose the answer that COMPLETES each sentence properly.

MODEL

Students _____ the TOEFL test to achieve university entrance have difficulty with this section.

(A) are taking
(B) who are take
(C) taking
(D) take

(A) This answer is incorrect. The main verb is *have*; there cannot be two main verbs in this sentence.
(B) This answer is incorrect. *Take* should be *taking*.
(C) This answer is correct. *Taking* is a reduced form of *who are taking*.
(D) This answer is incorrect. Like (A) above, there cannot be two main verbs in this sentence.

To answer this question, you must know about CLAUSES and PHRASES. Most questions in Part A test your knowledge of these two areas. This unit will help you recognize clauses and phrases and identify errors in their use.

Grammatical terms such as *clause, phrase, conjunction,* and *marker* are used to discuss the problems in Part A. You will be able to understand them by studying the examples and explanations in this unit. A summary of the grammar terms and further examples of them are located in Appendix B (page 145).

Special Note

Some students feel that they don't need to know the grammar rules of English to do well on Part A. They prefer to choose an answer by listening to the SOUND of the sentence as they put each answer choice in the blank.

However, it takes a lot of time to read up to four different versions of a sentence silently. Only fast readers can do this well. Also, sometimes the sound of an answer choice in a sentence may SEEM right, but actually it is not. Look at the Model; answers (A) and (D) both sound correct if you don't consider the grammar of the sentence carefully.

Listening silently to the sound of a sentence CAN be useful, but only when it is combined with an awareness of grammar rules.

Common Types of Problems

Certain types of grammar problems are likely to occur in Part A. Examples and explanations of these types are provided below. You should study each example carefully and try to choose the correct answer before you read the explanation.

• **The main clause is incomplete.**

1. _____ was an attempt to renew the classic architectural style of Greece and Rome.

   (A) It was the Gothic movement
   (B) While the Gothic movement
   (C) The Gothic movement
   (D) For the Gothic movement

   A MAIN CLAUSE is a sentence that is correct all by itself. A main clause must include at least a main subject and a main verb.

   In this example, the main subject is missing. Answer (C) contains the correct main subject.

2. Alcohol, long known to be a depressant drug, _____ activity in the central nervous system.

   (A) and lowers
   (B) lowers it
   (C) by lowering
   (D) lowers

   The main verb is missing. Answer (D) is the correct main verb. A phrase separates the main subject *alcohol* and the main verb.

3. Wildlife preserves _____ to protect species from extinction.

   (A) are intended
   (B) intend
   (C) intending
   (D) have intending

   A common problem with the main verb is whether it should have an active or passive form. (A) is in passive form, while (B) is in active form; (C) and (D) are not possible answers. Compare these sentences:

46

People *intend* wildlife preserves to protect endangered species. (active)
Wildlife preserves *are intended* (by people) to protect endangered species from extinction. (passive)

From this comparison you should see that (A) is correct. More explanation on the passive is in Appendix B (page 145).

4. _____ the automobile industry in the early 1900s.

  (A) It was Henry Ford's revolution
  (B) Henry Ford revolutionized
  (C) Revolutionized by Henry Ford
  (D) There was a revolution

Both a main subject and main verb are needed. (B) is correct because it contains these parts, and nothing more.

5. Of all the world's languages, _____.

  (A) dominating most business with English
  (B) the domination of business by English
  (C) English is the most dominant in business
  (D) when English dominates business

The entire main clause is missing. The correct answer is the one that has both a main subject and a main verb and that is correct by itself. (C) is the answer.

6. Most metals are rigid, _____ others are quite pliable.

  (A) like
  (B) there are
  (C) but
  (D) which

In this example, the clause marker is missing. A CLAUSE MARKER is a word used to join two sentences. The coordinating conjunction *but* is a clause marker that can join two main clauses. (C) is the correct answer.

• **The subordinate clause is incomplete.**

7. _____ birds are warm-blooded animals, they are not considered to be mammals.
  (A) Although
  (B) Many
  (C) How many
  (D) But

A SUBORDINATE CLAUSE is a sentence that is not correct by itself. It is always introduced by a clause marker and must contain at least a clause subject and a clause verb. The clause marker joins the main clause and subordinate clause.

In this example, the subordinate clause marker is missing. The subordinating conjunction *although* is a clause marker that can occur at the beginning of a sentence. (A) is the correct answer.

8. _____ seat belts save lives has been proven in study after study.

  (A) The
  (B) That
  (C) There are
  (D) If

Sometimes one sentence is the subject or object of a second sentence. *That* is a clause marker used to make a sentence the subject or object of another sentence.

In this example, the subordinate clause marker is missing again. The clause marker *that* is used to make the sentence *Seat belts save lives* the subject of the incomplete sentence, "...has been proven in study after study." (B) is correct.

9. Carpenter ants damage homes _____ chew through wood.

   (A) are they
   (B) when they
   (C) they
   (D) by they can

The main clause, *carpenter ants damage homes*, is complete. The word *chew* must be the verb in a subordinate clause. Therefore, a clause marker and subject are missing. The subordinating conjunction *when* is a clause marker that can join two sentences. (B) is correct.

10. Jet streams are layers of air _____ rapidly above the earth's surface.

   (A) that they move
   (B) move
   (C) that move
   (D) moving that

The relative pronoun *that* is a clause marker used to make one sentence describe part of another sentence (like an adjective). Compare these sentences:

1. Jet streams are layers of air.
2. The layers move rapidly above the earth's surface.
3. Jet streams are layers of air that move rapidly above the earth's surface.

The clause marker *that* replaces *the layers* in sentence 2, and sentences 1 and 2 are joined together to form sentence 3.

In this example, the clause marker (which is also the clause subject) and the clause verb are missing. The correct answer is (C).

11. At the early age of five, Albert Einstein was already wondering _____.

   (A) that a compass worked
   (B) with a compass working
   (C) having worked a compass
   (D) how a compass worked

An INFORMATION WORD is used to ask about something that is not known. An information word can make one sentence the subject or object of another sentence.

In this example, the entire subordinate clause is missing. The information word *how* is a clause marker introducing the subordinate clause. The subordinate clause is the object of the main clause. (D) is the correct answer.

• **The prepositional phrase is incomplete.**

12. _____ breakdown of the ozone layer, humans face increasing danger from exposure to the sun's rays.

   (A) Because the
   (B) Sometimes the
   (C) With the
   (D) The

The main clause starts after the comma. The first part does not contain a verb, so it cannot be a subordinate clause. Therefore, a clause marker is not needed.

A PHRASE is a set of words that does NOT have both a subject and a verb. A phrase always begins with a phrase marker. A preposition is a common phrase marker.

In this example, the first part is a phrase. The phrase needs to begin with a prepositional phrase marker. (C) is correct because it begins with the preposition *with*.

13. Katherine Anne Porter is well known _____.

    (A) for her short stories about young women
    (B) writing short stories about young women
    (C) short stories about women
    (D) she has written short stories about young women

In this case, the entire prepositional phrase is needed. (A) starts with the preposition *for* and is followed by a noun phrase; it is the correct answer.

14. Some animals, like the opossum, protect themselves from their enemies _____ to be dead.

    (A) their pretending
    (B) that they pretend
    (C) by pretending
    (D) the pretense

A prepositional phrase marker can be followed by a gerund (a noun formed from a verb). In this example, (C) is correct because it tells us HOW animals protect themselves.

* **The participial phrase is incomplete.**

15. Mach numbers describe the velocity of airplanes _____ over the speed of sound.

    (A) moved
    (B) moving
    (C) have moved
    (D) move

The main clause is *Mach numbers describe the velocity of airplanes*. The last part is a prepositional phrase. In this example, however, something is needed to explain what airplanes DO near the speed of sound.

This could be done by adding a clause beginning with a relative pronoun. The sentence would then be, ''Mach numbers describe the velocity of airplanes <u>which are moving</u> near the speed of sound.'' However, this is not one of the answer choices.

It is possible to take out *which are*, leaving the present participial form *moving*. In this example, *moving* is a present participial phrase marker. (B) is the correct answer.

NOTE: In the Model at the beginning of this unit, the correct answer is also a present participial phrase marker.

16. Hieroglyphics _____ on the walls of caves provide scientists with important details on prehistoric man.

    (A) that they painted
    (B) were painted
    (C) have been painted
    (D) painted

The main clause is ''Hieroglyphics . . . provide scientists with important details on prehistoric man.'' The middle part could be completed with a clause starting with a relative pronoun. The sentence would then be, "Hieroglyphics <u>which were painted</u> on the walls of caves give scientists..." However, this is not one of the answer choices.

Like 15, it is possible to take out *which were*, leaving the past participial form *painted*. A past participial form is the *-ed* form of a verb (except in the case of irregular verbs). In this example, *painted* is a past participial phrase marker. (D) is the correct answer.

- **The word order is wrong.**

17. Auroras are created when the sun's particles are caught in _____.

   (A) field the earth's magnetic
   (B) the magnetic earth's field
   (C) the field magnetic earth
   (D) the earth's magnetic field

   A noun phrase usually follows a preposition. A noun phrase must contain at least one noun, which may be preceded by an article (*a, an, the*) and/or adjectives.

   In this example, (D) provides the correct order for the noun phrase. The article is first, then the possessive form, then the adjective, and finally the noun. (B) is wrong because the field is magnetic, not the earth.

18. Asia _____ by most experts to be the cradle of human civilization.

   (A) has always been considered
   (B) has been always considered
   (C) always has been considered
   (D) has been considered always

   A verb phrase must contain a verb, and may have auxiliaries (words that help the verb) like *have* and *been* and adverbs (words that modify the verb) like *always*.

   In this example, (A) provides the correct order for a verb phrase. Adverbs such as *always* are placed after the first auxiliary (*has*).

19. Arabic and Swahili are _____ any other language of Africa.

   (A) more spoken widely than
   (B) widely spoken more than
   (C) more than widely spoken
   (D) more widely spoken than

   Comparative forms begin with *more* or *less* and end with *than*. Therefore, only (A) and (D) are possible. (D) is the correct answer because the adverb *widely* must precede the past participle form *spoken*.

20. Not only _____ resulted in vast expense, but they have endangered human existence as well.

   (A) have nuclear weapons
   (B) nuclear weapons have
   (C) will nuclear weapons
   (D) nuclear weapons that

   If a sentence begins with a term that has a negative meaning, then the sentence must be in QUESTION form. In this example, a question form is made by moving the auxiliary *have* in front of the subject. (A) is the correct answer.

   Note that the sentence ends with *as well*. You may be most familiar with the form "not only...but also..." An alternate form is "not only...but...as well."

50

21. Seldom _____ art critics consider movies to be a form of fine art.

    (A) are
    (B) do
    (C) that
    (D) the

Seldom is another negative word that requires a question form at the beginning of a sentence. In this case, however, the auxiliary *do* must be added to the sentence to form the question. (B) is the correct answer.

NOTE: Examples and explanations of all the negative forms used in initial position are in Appendix B (page 145).

22. The Grand Canyon, _____, is located in northwestern Arizona.

    (A) is one of the eight wonders of the world
    (B) having the eighth wonder of the world
    (C) it is one of the world's eight wonders
    (D) one of the eight wonders of the world

An APPOSITIVE is a noun phrase that helps to define another noun phrase. If it occurs after the subject, it is usually separated by commas.

In this example, the entire appositive phrase is missing. The correct answer is (D).

23. Sumerians were the first to invent cuneiform, _____.

    (A) which a system of writing
    (B) was a system of writing
    (C) a system of writing
    (D) for a system of writing

An appositive can also occur at the end of the sentence. In this example, the appositive form defines what *cuneiform* is. (C) is the correct answer.

• **An item in parallel structure is missing.**

24. The major forms of three-dimensional art include architecture, jewelry, and _____.

    (A) making sculptures
    (B) sculpture
    (C) sculptures are made
    (D) sculpture making

The requirement that all items in a series have the same grammatical form is referred to as PARALLEL STRUCTURE. In this example, the words *architecture* and *jewelry* are both nouns, so the third item in the series must also be a noun. (B) is the correct answer.

25. The faster the processing speed, the greater _____ provided by a computer.

    (A) the power
    (B) power is
    (C) is the power
    (D) power which is

The two parts of this sentence begin with special comparative forms that must be followed by noun phrases. (A) is the correct answer because it maintains parallel structure.

26. All scientists follow the same basic research principles as they pose questions, consider possible answers, and _____.

(A) with gathering evidence
(B) evidence is gathered
(C) gather evidence
(D) evidence gathers there

The third item in the list of verb phrases must be in parallel structure with the first two items. (C) is the correct answer because *gather* is the same present tense verb form as *pose* and *consider*.

Strategies for Part A

- You should not read the instructions for Part A. Like the Listening Comprehension section, the instructions are the same for every TOEFL exam. Instead, you should start working right away on the problems.

- One approach to solving a problem in Part A is to:
  1. listen to the sound of the sentence as you read it silently; and
  2. look at the answer choices and select one that best completes the sentence.

  This approach works well if the grammar of the sentence is rather simple or the answer choices are quite short.

- In the case of more complicated or longer problems, you should use a second approach:
  1. determine what parts of grammar are already in the sentence; and
  2. determine what parts of grammar are needed to complete the sentence properly.

- The steps to solving a problem by using the second approach are:
  1. Locate the subject and verb of the MAIN CLAUSE. If either or both are missing, look for them in the answers. If the main clause is fine, then go to Step 2.
  2. Check to see if there is a SUBORDINATE CLAUSE. If there is, locate the clause marker, subject, and verb. If any of these is missing, look for it in the answers. If there is no subordinate clause, or the clause is fine, then go to step 3.
  3. Check to see if there is any kind of PHRASE. If so, locate the phrase marker. If any part of the phrase is missing, then locate it in the answer choices.

- If you are not certain that an answer is correct, glance at the other answer choices to find which are definitely wrong. PROCESS OF ELIMINATION helps you limit the number of possible answers, which increases your chances.

  For example, choosing from four possible answers, your chances are 25 percent. If you eliminate one answer as impossible, your chances increase to 33 percent. Eliminate two answers, and your chances are 50 percent. Of course, if you eliminate three answers, then your chances are 100 percent.

- Do not waste time on a difficult problem. You have an average of 40 seconds for each problem. Some will be easier to solve and others will be more difficult, but you shouldn't spend more than about a minute on any single problem. Make a good guess and continue to the next one.

Structure Practice

This exercise provides practice in recognizing common grammar problems in Part A. Try to complete it within 10 minutes.

Directions: Questions 1–15 contain sentences that are incomplete in some way. You choose the ONE answer that completes each sentence properly.

Example I

The horizon appears to be curved when viewed _____ a high place.

(A) with
(B) from
(C) on
(D) out of

The sentence should read, "The horizon appears to be curved when viewed from a high place." Therefore, (B) is the correct answer.

Example II

_____ the meaning of vocabulary from context is an important skill.

(A) Determining
(B) Having determined
(C) It is determined
(D) Determination

The sentence should read, "Determining the meaning of vocabulary from context is an important skill." Therefore, (A) is the correct answer.

Now begin work on the questions.

1. After the seventh month of pregnancy, _____ a good chance of survival.

(A) it has a premature baby
(B) does a premature baby have
(C) there is a premature baby
(D) a premature baby has

2. A ballad, _____, is a song that tells a dramatic story.

(A) for the oldest form of poetry
(B) which the oldest form of poetry
(C) the oldest form of poetry
(D) is the oldest form of poetry

GO ON TO THE NEXT PAGE

53

3. The decline in the death rate among babies can be attributed to advances in medicine, public health, and _____.

   (A) food production
   (B) producing food
   (C) food is produced
   (D) for the production of food

4. Rarely _____ succeed in ballet if they start after the age of 12.

   (A) children
   (B) children have
   (C) do children
   (D) are children

5. _____ can cause diseases such as tuberculosis by entering openings in the body.

   (A) Bacteria is harmful when
   (B) Harmful bacteria
   (C) Where harmful bacteria
   (D) If bacteria is harmful,

6. Migratory patterns in birds _____ terms of seasonal changes.

   (A) can usually be explained in
   (B) can be explained in usually
   (C) in usually can be explained
   (D) can be explained usually in

7. Babies often sleep up to 23 hours per day _____.

   (A) that is in the first month of life
   (B) during the first month of life
   (C) when the first month of life
   (D) for it is the first month of life

8. Radiocarbon dating is still the most common way of determining the age of human remains, _____ it is not always accurate.

   (A) in that
   (B) even though
   (C) when
   (D) that

9. Eugene O'Neill, a famous American dramatist, _____ the theater by using controversial themes and new stage techniques.

   (A) he revolutionized
   (B) there was a revolution in
   (C) revolutionized
   (D) in revolutionizing

10. Louis Renault greatly improved automobile technology _____ the drive shaft in 1898.

    (A) by inventing
    (B) that he invented
    (C) his inventing
    (D) the invention of

11. _____ the process of photosynthesis, green plants absorb carbon dioxide and produce oxygen.

    (A) That is
    (B) Through
    (C) It is
    (D) While

12. During the Period of Enlightenment, most philosophers _____ learning truth by reasoning.

    (A) were stressed
    (B) stressing
    (C) stressed
    (D) have been stressed

GO ON TO THE NEXT PAGE ➤

13. _____ animals can change colors to match their surroundings is an amazing fact of nature.

(A) If
(B) That
(C) The
(D) There are

14. The first use of advertising is believed to be signs, _____ above the doors of commercial businesses in Greece and Rome.

(A) which were posted
(B) having posted
(C) which posted
(D) posting

15. Air consists of a combination of nitrogen and oxygen _____ in place by gravity.

(A) are holding
(B) being hold
(C) holding
(D) held

Explanations and Answers for Structure Practice

1. (D). The main clause is not complete. The main subject and main verb are missing.
2. (C). An appositive phrase is needed to explain what a ballad is. (D) is wrong because the main clause already contains the verb *is*.
3. (A). This is a problem in parallel structure. *Medicine* and *public health* are both noun phrases; a third noun phrase is needed.
4. (C). When a main clause begins with a negative word such as *rarely*, a question form is needed. (D) is wrong because the auxiliary *do* is used with the present tense.
5. (B). The main clause is not complete. A main subject is needed.
6. (A). This is a problem of word order in the missing verb phrase. Adverbs are usually placed after the first auxiliary (*can*).
7. (B). The sentence is best completed by a prepositional phrase.
8. (B). There are two sentences. The relationship between the sentences is that of CONTRAST. The first is the main clause. The second is part of a subordinate clause, so a clause marker is needed.
9. (C). The main clause is not complete. The main verb is missing. (A) is wrong because there would be a double subject (*Eugene O'Neill* and *he*).
10. (A). A phrase or clause marker is needed after the main clause. Both (A) and (B) start with markers, but (B) is wrong because *that* is not used as a relative pronoun.
11. (B). The first part is either a phrase or a subordinate clause. Because "the process of photosynthesis" is a noun phrase, not a sentence, a phrase marker is needed.
12. (C). This is a problem of active or passive form for the main verb. *Learning truth* is an object, so the verb must be active.
13. (B). The first part is a sentence that is the SUBJECT of another sentence (the main verb is *is*). The sentence is a statement of fact.
14. (A). This is a very difficult problem. First, (D) is wrong because signs cannot post anything; PEOPLE post signs. Therefore, a passive form is needed in the blank. A relative pronoun should be used to connect the first part of the sentence to the second part.
15. (D). A past participle is used here to connect the first part of the sentence to the second part. Originally the sentence was "... nitrogen and oxygen, which are held in place..." This form can be reduced, leaving the past participle *held*. This same process could be done to 14 ("... signs posted ...").

Written Expression (Part B)

In Part B you will read sentences that are INCORRECT in some way. You will choose the one underlined part that is WRONG.

MODEL

Students in intensive language institutes study many subjects such as English vocabulary,
       A   B   C

grammar, and how to read.
          D

To answer this question, you must know about parallel structure, one of the areas tested in this section as well as in Part A. The answer is (D) because a noun form is needed.

Common Types of Problems

This section will help you to recognize common problems in Part B. Generally, problems occur in the following areas:

Word Choice and Word Form
Prepositions
Parallel Structure
Redundancy

Agreement
Missing or Double Subject
Word Order
Article Usage

Examples and explanations of these problems are provided below. You should study each example carefully and try to choose the correct answer before you read the explanation.

- **The choice of word is incorrect.**

  1. A company <u>who</u> advertises <u>extensively on</u> television generally <u>experiences</u> a large
           A   B   C

     increase <u>in revenues</u>.
              D

     The wrong relative pronoun is used. The relative pronoun *who* is used for people, NOT organizations such as a company. (A) is wrong. The correct answer is *that*.

  2. <u>University</u> administrators can <u>dismiss any</u> untenured faculty member <u>which</u> is not
         A   B   C

     fulfilling <u>his or her</u> duties.
             D

     The relative pronoun *which* is used for things, NOT people. (C) is wrong. The correct answer is *who*.

  3. <u>The milk</u> of <u>both goats</u> and cows <u>can be</u> used <u>to do</u> dairy products.
         A   B   C   D

     The wrong verb is used. The verb *to do* is used for performing some action, NOT for creating new items. (D) is wrong. The correct answer is *to make*.

  4. <u>Generally</u>, <u>tropical</u> areas <u>have</u> very humid and are <u>well suited</u> to heavy vegetation.
         A   B   C   D

     The verb *to have* is used with noun phrases, NOT adjective phrases such as *very humid*. (C) is wrong. The correct answer is *are*.

  5. <u>Because</u> their <u>rapid reproductive</u> rate, bacteria can <u>be grown</u> easily <u>in a</u> laboratory
         A   B   C   D

     setting.

     The wrong marker is used. A clause marker such as *because* is used before sentences, NOT before noun phrases. (A) is wrong. The correct answer is the phrase marker *because of*.

  6. <u>Ballet takes</u> years of <u>practice to</u> master, <u>therefore</u> children begin study <u>as early as</u> eight
           A   B   C   D

     years old.

     The clause marker *therefore* occurs after a semicolon (;) or period (.), NOT a comma. (C) is wrong. The correct answer is the clause marker *so*, which occurs after a comma.

7. <u>Army ants</u> are <u>too</u> ferocious that they <u>are capable</u> of <u>killing and eating</u> larger animals.
      A   B   C   D

There is no conjunctive form "too...that." (B) is wrong. The correct answer is *so*, which is needed to create the conjunctive form "so...that."

8. Clara Barton, <u>who</u> was <u>devoted with</u> nursing for <u>most</u> of her life, <u>founded the</u> American
                A   B   C   D
Red Cross.

The wrong preposition is used. The verb *devote* is always used with the preposition *to*. (B) is wrong. The correct answer is *devoted to*.

9. <u>The Universal</u> Product Code is a bar code <u>consisting</u> 11 numbers <u>as well as</u> bars and lines .
        A   B   C   D

The verb *consist* takes the preposition *of*. (B) is wrong; it should be *consisting of*.

NOTE: A list of common adjective/preposition and verb/preposition combinations can be found in Appendix B (page 145).

10. <u>Agriculture</u> , the <u>farming of</u> land, is <u>the world's</u> most important <u>industrialization</u> .
        A   B   C   D

The wrong noun form is used. The term *industrialization* refers to the act of MAKING an industry. (D) is wrong. The correct answer is *industry*.

- **The form of the word is incorrect.**

11. Australia <u>is a</u> <u>largely unexplored</u> country <u>having</u> vast mineral <u>wealths</u> .
               A   B   C   D

The wrong noun form is used. Certain nouns cannot be counted; they are called UNCOUNTABLE NOUNS. (D) is wrong. The correct answer is *wealth*.

12. <u>Most</u> <u>undergraduate students</u> find <u>mathematic</u> courses <u>to be among</u> the most difficult.
       A   B   C   D

Certain nouns referring to academic subjects appear to be plural, but are not. (C) is wrong. The correct answer is *mathematics*.

13. The <u>most natural</u> form of <u>nutrition</u> for newborn <u>infant</u> is <u>breast feeding</u> .
            A   B   C   D

This sentence refers to all infants, not just one. (C) is wrong. The correct answer is *infants*.

NOTE: A list of some common countable and uncountable nouns can be found in Appendix B (page 145).

14. <u>Anthropology</u> Margaret Mead <u>was famous</u> for <u>her study</u> of <u>adolescence</u> in Samoa.
         A   B   C   D

The term *anthropology* refers to a field of study, not a person who works in the field. To refer to a person, the suffix *-ist* is needed. (A) is wrong. The correct answer is *anthropologist*.

15. The cotton gin's inventing was the main factor behind the agricultural revolution of the
    <u>A</u>   <u>B</u>   <u>C</u>   <u>D</u>
    1700s.

    The proper suffix for the subject in this sentence is *-tion*. (B) is wrong. The correct answer
    is *invention*.

NOTE: A list of common suffixes can be found in Appendix B (page 145).

16. <u>Physicists are</u> scientists <u>whose</u> study matter <u>and energy</u>, as well <u>as their</u> patterns of
       <u>A</u>   <u>B</u>   <u>C</u>   <u>D</u>
    interaction.

    The wrong pronoun form is used. The possessive form of the relative pronoun *whose* is
    inappropriate. (B) is wrong. The correct answer is *who*.

17. Among <u>present-day</u> art critics, <u>French artist</u> Theodore Rousseau <u>was considered</u> <u>to be</u> the
             <u>A</u>   <u>B</u>   <u>C</u>   <u>D</u>
    most influential member of the Barbizon School.

    The wrong verb form is used. The term *present-day* indicates that the time is NOW, so the
    main verb should be in the present tense. (C) is wrong. The correct answer is *is considered*.

18. Since <u>the early</u> 1900s, the <u>most popular</u> indoor <u>sport played</u> in America <u>was</u> basketball.
            <u>A</u>   <u>B</u>   <u>C</u>   <u>D</u>

    The time word *since* is a phrase marker that requires a main verb in the present perfect
    tense. (D) is wrong. The correct answer is *has been*.

19. Sociologists <u>are trying</u> to predict the quality <u>of life</u> in urban areas in <u>the year</u> 2000 if
                    <u>A</u>   <u>B</u>   <u>C</u>
    present trends <u>will continue</u>.
                     <u>D</u>

    If is a clause marker introducing a future condition clause. The verb in a future condition
    clause must be in simple present tense. (D) is wrong; the correct answer is *continue*.

    The simple present tense must also be used in future time clauses. Clause markers such as
    when, before, after, and *as soon as* are used to introduce future time clauses.

20. Bears <u>are usually</u> peaceful <u>animals that</u> attack <u>only when</u> they are <u>provocation</u>.
            <u>A</u>   <u>B</u>   <u>C</u>   <u>D</u>

    The pronoun *they* refers to bears. The following verb should be in passive form. (D) is
    wrong. The correct answer is *provoked*.

21. P. T. Barnum, <u>the famous</u> circus owner, <u>was the</u> most <u>prominence</u> showman <u>of his time</u>.
                     <u>A</u>   <u>B</u>   <u>C</u>   <u>D</u>

    The wrong descriptive form is used. The noun *showman* should be preceded by an
    adjective, not a noun. (C) is wrong. The correct answer is *prominent*.

22. John Barrymore <u>was critical</u> <u>acclaimed</u> for his <u>dynamic</u> performance as the
                      <u>A</u>   <u>B</u>   <u>C</u>
    Shakespearean <u>character</u> Hamlet.
                    <u>D</u>

Only an adverb can be placed between an auxiliary such as *be* or *have* and a past participle such as *acclaimed*. (A) is wrong. The correct answer is *was critically*.

- **Parallel structure is not maintained.**

23. The Basques of the Pyrenees are famous for their unique language, colorful costumes,
    A   B   C
    and fierce independent.
              D

   The list of three items for which Basques are famous must have the same grammatical form. Because *language* and *customs* are both nouns, the third item must also be a noun. (D) is wrong. The correct answer is *independence*.

24. New York is home to some of the most famous artistic and theater productions
    A   B   C
    in the world.
    D

   The noun *productions* should be preceded by adjectives. *Artistic* is an adjective, *theater* is not. (C) is wrong. The correct answer is *theatrical*.

25. A worker bee is a female that does chores and taking care of the young in a bee colony.
    A   B   C   D

   The verbs *do* and *take* should be in parallel structure. (C) is wrong; it should be *takes*.

26. Barbiturates are drugs that are used to calm people or making them sleep.
    A   B   C   D

   The gerund *making* is not in parallel structure with the infinitive *to calm*. Since the infinitive is not underlined, the gerund should be changed. (C) is wrong. The correct answer is *to make*.

- **Redundant forms are used.**

27. The Alaskan bear, averaging nine feet tall, is the very largest of all meat-eating land
    A   B   C   D
    animals.

   The superlative form *largest* means *most large*. Since *very* and *most* are similar in meaning (REDUNDANT), they should not occur together. (C) is wrong. The word *very* should be removed.

28. The invention of the laser greatly expanded the power of scientific research
    A   B   C
    tremendously.
    D

   The adverbs *greatly* and *tremendously* mean the same thing. (D) is wrong. *Tremendously* should be removed.

- **The article usage is incorrect.**

29. <u>An art</u> of barbering, now <u>commonly called</u> hairdressing, <u>requires</u> formal <u>licensing of</u> its

  A   B   C   D
    practitioners.

    A noun followed by a prepositional phrase is usually preceded by a definite article. (A) is wrong. The correct answer is *the art*.

30. Mikhail Baryshnikov, one of <u>world's</u> <u>foremost ballet</u> <u>dancers</u>, defected <u>to the West</u> in

                                    A   B   C   D
    1974.

    A noun preceded by *one of* usually occurs with a definite article. (A) is wrong. The correct answer is *of the world's*.

- **The order of words is incorrect.**

31. The process <u>by which</u> bees <u>sting requires</u> the <u>use of</u> 25 <u>muscles different</u>.

                 A   B   C   D

    An adjective precedes the noun it modifies. (D) is wrong. The correct answer is *different muscles*.

32. <u>Mushrooms thrive</u> in damp places, <u>where</u> <u>is there</u> plenty of <u>moisture and</u> nutrients.

        A   B   C   D

    The term *where* does not introduce a question form in this sentence, so the subject *there* should precede the verb *is*. (C) is wrong. The correct answer is *there is*.

- **The subject form is incorrect.**

33. Bedouins, <u>Arab people</u> living in the <u>deserts</u> of the Middle East, <u>they</u> are

                A   B   C
    <u>nomadic tribesmen</u>.

      D

    The main subject is *bedouins*; the main verb is *are*. The pronoun *they* refers to *bedouins*, thus creating a double subject. (C) is wrong; it should be removed.

34. Alexander Graham <u>Bell figured</u> out <u>a way to</u> transmit <u>speech</u> electronically <u>when was</u>

                            A   B   C   D
    just 27.

    The clause introduced by *when* should contain a subject as well as a verb. (D) is wrong. The correct answer is *when he was*.

- **Sentence forms are not in agreement.**

35. People who <u>use drugs</u> extensively <u>to relieve</u> tension often <u>experiences</u> painful withdrawal

              A   B   C
    <u>when trying</u> to stop.

     D

61

The main subject *people* is plural, so the main verb should be plural. (C) is wrong. The correct answer is *experience*.

36. The <u>owners</u> of a commercial <u>bank are</u> comprised of stockholders <u>who have</u> shares <u>in them</u> .
        A   B   C   D

Stockholders have shares in a bank. A pronoun referring to *bank* should be singular. (D) is wrong. The correct answer is *in it*.

NOTE: Examples 35 and 36 are difficult because the subject/verb and noun/pronoun are separated by many words. It is easy to forget to check for agreement.

Strategies for Part B

- Once again, you should not take time to read the instructions. Start working on the problems immediately.

- One key to doing well in Part B is the ability to recognize the problem areas listed above.

- The steps in choosing the incorrect answer choice are:

  1. Read the sentence quickly, paying special attention to the four underlined parts.
  2. If you are certain that you have identified the problem, mark the appropriate answer and move on to the next question.
  3. If you have any doubt about what the problem is, compare the underlined parts with other parts of the sentence.

  This last point is very important if you cannot find any problem with the underlined parts. Sometimes the problem can be noticed only in relationship to other parts of the sentence. An obvious example of this is subject-verb agreement, as in 35 above.

- In Part B, paying attention to the SOUND of a sentence as you read it silently is always a good strategy. Unlike Part A, there are no choices to put into a blank, and you are trying to find what is WRONG, not right. In such a case, listening to the sound of the sentence can help.

- The most common areas tested in Part B are WORD CHOICE and WORD FORM problems. The reason is that knowledge of these areas is hard to teach and comes only after years of practice in English. One area of help to you, however, is the set of suffixes that are added to words to create different grammatical forms. You should continue to review the ones listed in Appendix B (page 145).

- Another common area tested is PREPOSITION usage, for the same reason given above. There are certain combinations involving adjectives and verbs that you should know. You should continue to review the ones listed in Appendix B (page 145).

Written Expression Practice

This exercise provides practice in recognizing common problems in written expression. Try to complete it within 15 minutes.

Directions: Questions 1–25 contain sentences that are incorrect in some way. You choose the one underlined part that is wrong.

Example I

Particles of salt dissolved in water retains their salinity.
   A   B   C   D

The sentence should read, "Particles of salt dissolved in water retain their salinity." Therefore, (C) is the proper choice.

Example II

The emissions from a diesel-powered automobile are not as dangerous as
      A   B

that from a gasoline-powered vehicle.
C   D

The sentence should read, "The emissions from a diesel-powered automobile are not as dangerous as those from a gasoline-powered vehicle." Therefore, (C) is the proper choice.

Now begin work on the questions.

1. Teachers who give a lot of homeworks are generally better regarded by their
     A   B   C
students than those who don't.
       D

2. The most important playwright of the postwar period was Tennessee
     A   B   C
Williams, whom wrote *The Glass Menagerie.*
      D

3. The discovery of gold in the Klondike attracted thousands interested in
      A   B   C
doing a fortune.
  D

4. Most major companies maintain large advertising budgets so that can
             A   B
compete successfully against other companies.
  C   D

5. The <u>first electronic</u> computer <u>components</u> <u>were inventing</u> in the <u>early 1950s</u>.
    A   B   C   D

6. Heavy withdrawals on <u>bank resources</u>, known <u>as run</u>, <u>caused the</u> Great
                     A   B   C

   Depression <u>of the</u> 1930s.
         D

7. An infant child <u>notices and pays attention</u> to <u>more stimuli</u> than <u>was</u>
               A   B   C

   previously <u>thought</u>.
        D

8. Walter <u>Gropius was</u> the <u>founding</u> of the <u>famous school</u> of design <u>called the</u>
        A   B   C   D

   Bauhaus.

9. <u>Western nations</u> have <u>considered always</u> communist countries <u>to be</u>
     A   B   C

   <u>enemies of</u> democracy.
  D

10. <u>Many charitable</u> organizations <u>are devoted</u> <u>for eliminating</u> poverty and
    A   B   C

   <u>illiteracy in</u> the United States.
   D

11. Batteries <u>are used</u> as <u>a ready</u> source of <u>electricity in</u> various forms of
         A   B   C

   <u>portable equipped</u>.
   D

12. <u>During trade</u> was <u>initiated with</u> Chinese and Japanese <u>feudal lords</u> in the
    A   B   C

   nineteenth century, <u>the colonial</u> period begin in Asia.
                D

13. There <u>are nearly</u> 10,000 <u>bee species</u> that <u>exists in</u> most parts of <u>the world</u>.
       A   B   C   D

14. Plant <u>species of</u> the <u>northern hemisphere</u> differ <u>greatly between</u> those <u>of the</u>
       A   B   C   D

   southern hemisphere.

15. The state of California, a <u>recognized leader</u> in agriculture and manufacturing,
                       A

   <u>it has</u> a gross national <u>product that</u> is larger <u>than that</u> of most countries.
  B   C   D

GO ON TO THE NEXT PAGE ►

16. Natural-born artists <u>have an</u> innate ability to <u>creative images</u> in their minds
       A   B   C

    <u>with little</u> effort.
      D

17. The <u>ingredients used</u> to prepare <u>many</u> food items are <u>trade secrets</u> of the
          A   B   C

    companies that <u>sell it</u>.
               D

18. The <u>great deep</u> and width <u>of the</u> Grand Canyon <u>make it</u> a spectacular
        A   B   C

    <u>natural attraction</u>.
         D

19. The discovery of the <u>nuclear fission</u> process <u>was one of</u> the most
                  A   B

    <u>important breakthroughs</u> in the field <u>of physic</u>.
             C   D

20. <u>Fungi</u> grow <u>best</u> when <u>is there</u> a lot of <u>moisture available</u>.
     A   B   C   D

21. On the average, <u>incidents</u> of family crime are <u>generally</u> <u>unreported</u> to
                  A   B   C

    <u>authorities</u>.
      D

22. Martin Luther <u>King was</u> <u>an important</u> academic, <u>politics</u>, and intellectual
             A   B   C

    <u>leader in</u> America.
       D

23. The <u>rate of</u> juvenile delinquency <u>is related</u> the high school <u>dropout</u> rate
        A   B   C

    <u>in a community</u>.
        D

24. Titanium is a metal that is <u>too strong</u> that <u>it is</u> very <u>useful for</u> military
                        A   B   C

    <u>applications.</u>
       D

25. Commercial businesses <u>whose purchase</u> advertising time on
                      A

    <u>television experience</u> a <u>substantial</u> increase <u>in product</u> sales.
           B   C   D

Explanations and Answers for Written Expression Practice

1. (B). An uncountable noun cannot be made plural. The correct answer is *of homework are*.
2. (D). A subject pronoun form should precede the verb *wrote*. The correct answer is *who*.
3. (D). *Do* is for activity, *make* is for producing or acquiring something, such as a fortune. The correct answer is *making*.
4. (B). A subject pronoun is needed after the clause marker and before the verb phrase *can compete*. The correct answer is *so that they*.
5. (C). The verb must be in passive form, so a past participle is needed. The correct answer is *were invented*.
6. (B). An indefinite article is needed to modify the noun *run*. The correct answer is *as a run*.
7. (A). The verbs *to notice* and *to pay attention* mean the same thing, so it is redundant to include both of them. The correct answer is *notices* or *pays attention*.
8. (B). Walter Gropius was the person who founded the Bauhaus. The correct answer is *founder*.
9. (B) An adverb should follow an auxiliary form. The correct answer is *always considered*.
10. (C). The proper verb/preposition combination is *to be devoted to*. The correct answer is *to eliminating*.
11. (D). A noun form is needed after an adjective. The correct answer is *portable equipment*.
12. (A). A clause marker, not the phrase marker *during*, is needed. The correct answer is *when trade*.
13. (C). The relative pronoun *that* refers to the plural form *species*, so the clause verb must be plural. This is a problem of subject-verb agreement. The correct answer is *exist in*.
14. (C). The proper verb/preposition combination is *to differ from*. The correct answer is *greatly from*.
15. (B). The subject is *the state of California*, so another pronoun subject cannot occur. The correct answer is *has*.
16. (C). It should be *create images*. An infinitive verb form, not an adjective form, is needed.
17. (D). The pronoun refers to *food items*, which is plural. This is a problem of noun-pronoun agreement. The correct answer is *sell them*.
18. (A). The adjective *deep* is not in parallel structure with the noun *width*. The correct answer is *great depth*.
19. (D). *Physics* is an uncountable noun that ends in *-ics*. The correct answer is *of physics*.
20. (C). A question form is not used after the clause marker *when*. The correct answer is *when there is*.
21. (B). The beginning phrase *on the average* means *generally*, so (B) is redundant. (B) should be removed.
22. (C). The three adjectives modifying the noun *leader* must be in parallel structure. The correct answer is *political*.
23. (B). The verb *relate* occurs with the preposition *to*. The correct answer is *is related to*.
24. (A). The proper clause marker is "*so . . . that*." The correct answer is *so strong*.
25. (A). The relative pronoun must be a subject form. The correct answer is *that purchase*.

Structure Practice Test

SECTION 2

STRUCTURE AND WRITTEN EXPRESSION

Time—25 minutes

This section tests your ability to identify appropriate forms of formal written English. There are two parts to this section.

<u>Directions:</u> Questions 1–15 contain sentences that are incomplete in some way. You choose the ONE answer that completes each sentence properly.

Example I

The horizon appears to be curved when viewed _____ a high place.

(A) with
(B) from
(C) on
(D) out of

The sentence should read, "The horizon appears to be curved when viewed from a high place." Therefore, (B) is the correct answer.

Example II

_____ the meaning of vocabulary from context is an important skill.

(A) Determining
(B) Having determined
(C) It is determined
(D) Determination

The sentence should read, "Determining the meaning of vocabulary from context is an important skill." Therefore, (A) is the correct answer.

Now begin work on the questions.

GO ON TO THE NEXT PAGE

1. Supersonic flight is flight faster than the speed of sound, which ------------ Mach 1.

   (A) calling
   (B) is called
   (C) has been calling
   (D) called

2. Of all the countries of the world, ------------.

   (A) the U.S. allocation of the most funds for advertising
   (B) the most funds for advertising allocated in the U.S.
   (C) the U.S. allocates the most funds for advertising
   (D) allocating the most funds for advertising in the U.S.

3. The principal basis of the scientific method is careful observation and ------------.

   (A) doing experiments
   (B) experimental designing
   (C) experiments are done
   (D) experimentation

4. The Alaskan Highway, ------------ between Alaska and the continental U.S., runs more than 1,400 miles along the west coast of North America.

   (A) is the main artery
   (B) that the main artery
   (C) the main artery
   (D) it is the main artery

5. The blue whale ------------ the largest creature on earth.

   (A) generally classified as is
   (B) as is generally classified
   (C) is generally classified as
   (D) is classified generally as

6. Henry Aaron hit more home runs during his career ------------ any other player in baseball history.

   (A) as
   (B) from
   (C) than
   (D) despite

7. Some animals nurture their young ------------ leave their offspring to survive on their own.

   (A) while others
   (B) in spite of others
   (C) if others
   (D) others having

8. ------------ one of the oldest art forms, combining beauty and functionality into one.

   (A) Because architecture is
   (B) Having architecture as
   (C) Architecture being
   (D) Architecture is

9. Artifacts are ancient objects ------------ an archeological site during excavation.

   (A) found in
   (B) which find
   (C) having found in
   (D) in the find of

10. Batik is the technique of putting colorful designs on fabric by covering portions with wax, dipping the cloth in dye, and ------------.

    (A) it is allowed to dry
    (B) allowed drying of it
    (C) have it dried
    (D) allowing it to dry

GO ON TO THE NEXT PAGE

11. It is still a mystery _____ worker bees in a hive know what to do or when to do it.

 (A) that
 (B) how
 (C) whether
 (D) however

12. The atmosphere _____ the earth is divided into four layers according to differences in temperature.

 (A) surrounded
 (B) of surrounding
 (C) is surrounded by
 (D) surrounding

13. The greater the repressive force, _____ the will of the people to rebel.

 (A) the stronger is
 (B) the strength of
 (C) is stronger
 (D) the stronger

14. Not only _____ useful in producing dairy products, but also it is used for rapid reproduction of bacteria in scientific research.

 (A) fermentation has been
 (B) is fermentation
 (C) does fermentation
 (D) fermentation is

15. _____ composers such as Mozart, who was treated as an employee by those who commissioned him, Beethoven enjoyed equal social status with his employers.

 (A) Because
 (B) There were
 (C) Unlike
 (D) Having been

Directions: Questions 16–40 contain sentences that are incorrect in some way. You choose the one underlined part that is wrong.

Example I

Particles of salt dissolved in water retains their salinity.
   A   B   C   D

The sentence should read, "Particles of salt dissolved in water retain their salinity." Therefore, (C) is the proper choice.

GO ON TO THE NEXT PAGE

Example II

The <u>emissions from</u> a diesel-powered automobile <u>are not as</u>
     A   B

dangerous as <u>that</u> from a <u>gasoline-powered</u> vehicle.
          C   D

The sentence should read, "The emissions from a diesel-powered automobile are not as dangerous as those from a gasoline-powered vehicle." Therefore, (C) is the proper choice.

Now begin work on the questions.

16. <u>Near all</u> of the sciences <u>are based</u> on mathematical <u>principles</u> <u>that help</u> to
    A   B   C   D
validate the investigative process.

17. Camp David, <u>the official</u> <u>retreat of</u> U.S. presidents, is located in an area
                 A   B
<u>where is there</u> <u>ample security</u>.
     C   D

18. The Renaissance <u>it was</u> a period <u>of rebirth</u> of <u>the classical</u> culture of Italy
                A   B   C
<u>during the</u> 1400s.
    D

19. <u>Although</u> agriculture is the <u>leading economics</u> activity in Africa, it is
   A   B
accomplished <u>almost exclusively</u> <u>with primitive</u> tools.
            C   D

20. <u>A mammal can</u> be <u>defined as</u> a warm-blooded <u>animal that</u> feeds <u>their babies</u>
         A   B   C   D
with mother's milk.

21. <u>Within</u> China, calligraphy <u>is considered</u> a <u>greatest art</u> form than <u>painting</u>.
   A   B   C   D

22. A <u>dirigible is</u> a gas-filled <u>balloon that</u> <u>can be navigating</u> by <u>engines and</u>
     A   B   C   D
propellers.

23. Julius Caesar, <u>appointed</u> dictator of Rome <u>for life</u>, abused his <u>power</u> and
           A   B   C
<u>alienating his</u> supporters.
    D

GO ON TO THE NEXT PAGE ➤

24. Animals <u>were first</u> domesticated for food, <u>and later</u> became <u>important with</u> a
      A   B   C
   source <u>of skin</u>, fur, and wool.
            D

25. <u>The</u> foundation of calculus <u>is laid</u> by <u>the famous</u> Greek <u>mathematician</u>
      A   B   C   D
   Archimedes.

26. Amphibians, <u>which live</u> both on land <u>or water</u>, have developed <u>specialized</u>
                   A   B   C
   apparatus <u>such as</u> webbed feet for movement in water.
                D

27. <u>Army ants</u> are <u>ferocious</u> fighters <u>capable for</u> killing and eating larger
      A   B   C
   <u>yet slower</u> animals.
      D

28. <u>The earliest</u> vehicles <u>were heavy</u>, steam-driven machines <u>producing</u>
      A   B   C
   <u>great amount</u> of noise and smoke.
      D

29. <u>The League</u> of Women Voters <u>is an</u> organization <u>who promotes</u> the active
      A   B   C
   <u>involvement of</u> women in public life.
      D

30. In <u>the transmission</u> of <u>communication</u> signals, pulses of energy in the form of
         A   B
   <u>light is</u> directed through <u>fiber optic</u> cables.
      C   D

31. Juan Rodriguez <u>Cabrillo led</u> the <u>first</u> Spanish <u>expedition to</u> explore
                       A   B   C
   <u>the coast in</u> California.
      D

32. <u>Locks are</u> required <u>in</u> canals <u>how changes</u> in terrain <u>occur</u>.
      A   B   C   D

33. <u>Like to</u> a cow, a camel does not chew <u>its food well</u> before <u>swallowing</u>, forcing
      A   B   C
   <u>it to</u> regurgitate the contents of its stomach at a later time.
      D

34. <u>One of the</u> main leaders of <u>the Protestant</u> Reformation, John Calvin,
      A   B
   <u>believed with</u> the participation of <u>the people</u> in political decision-making.
      C   D

GO ON TO THE NEXT PAGE ➤

71

35. The strong beat of <u>calypso</u> <u>does</u> it a <u>particularly</u> powerful form <u>of folk</u> music.
                           A   B   C   D

36. <u>An aperture</u> is a hole <u>through which</u> light enters <u>and passes into</u> <u>the body</u> of
    A   B   C   D

a camera.

37. <u>Laser equipments</u> can be <u>used to</u> remove bad <u>tissue from</u> the body or
    A   B   C

<u>to reattach</u> parts of the retina of the eye.
    D

38. <u>In its</u> most <u>general sensation</u>, art is <u>any skill</u> in <u>making</u> something.
    A   B   C   D

39. The Library <u>of Congress</u>, one of the <u>world's oldest</u> and most important
                A   B

research libraries, contains <u>above</u> 77 million items <u>ranging from</u> books to
                         C   D

photographs.

40. In 1930, <u>novelist</u> Sinclair Lewis <u>had become</u> the <u>first</u> American author <u>to win</u>
         A   B   C   D

the Nobel Prize.

Explanations and Answers begin on the following page.

Explanations and Answers for Structure Practice Test

Structure

1. (B). The subordinate clause (in this case, a relative clause) is not complete. A passive verb form is needed after the relative pronoun to maintain the proper meaning ("The speed of sound is called Mach 1").

2. (C). The entire main clause is missing. The correct answer contains a main subject (*The U.S.*) and a main verb (*allocates*).

3. (D). This is a problem of parallel structure involving the nouns *observation* and *experimentation*.

4. (C). The appositive form following the main subject is incomplete. An appositive must be a noun phrase.

5. (C). This is a problem of word order. An adverb is usually placed after the first auxiliary.

6. (C). The comparative form is "more . . . than."

7. (A). The clause marker and clause subject are missing. The correct answer contains both of these.

8. (D). The main clause is incomplete. A main subject and verb are needed.

9. (A). The past participle form *found* comes from reducing the clause *that are found*.

10. (D). This is a problem of parallel structure involving the present participle forms *covering*, *dipping*, and *allowing*.

11. (B). The clause marker is missing. An information word is needed here because the statement is about something unknown, not something factual. [If it were a fact, (A) would be correct.]

12. (D). A phrase marker is needed. A present participial form is appropriate because the atmosphere surrounds the earth (active form).

13. (D). This is a very special problem in parallel structure. Note that there is no main verb in this sentence.

14. (B). After an initial negative term, a question form is required. With an adjective such as *useful*, a form of *be* should be used.

15. (C). The main clause is at the end of the sentence. Therefore, a phrase marker is needed to introduce the initial noun phrase.

Written Expression

16. (A). The correct answer is *nearly all*.

17. (C). A question form is not appropriate here. The correct answer is *where there is*.

18. (A). This is a problem of double subject form. *It* should be removed.

19. (B). *Economics* is a noun form. The adjective form *economic* must be used. The correct answer is *leading economic*.

20. (D). The pronoun must agree in number with the preceding noun (*animal*). The correct answer is *its babies*.

21. (C). The comparative form "more . . . than" is needed. The correct answer is *greater art*.

22. (C). A passive verb form should be used. The correct answer is *can be navigated*.

23. (D). This is a problem of parallel structure involving verb forms. The correct answer is *alienated his*.

24. (C). The wrong preposition is used. The correct answer is *important as*.

25. (B). A past tense verb form is needed because Archimedes was an ancient Greek mathematician. The correct answer is *was laid*.

26. (B). The form *both* occurs with *and*. The correct answer is *and water*.

27. (C). The wrong preposition is used. The correct answer is *capable of*.

28. (D). The noun form *amount* is countable and should be plural. The correct answer is *great amounts*.

29. (C). The relative pronoun *who* is used for people, not organizations. The correct answer is *that promotes*.

30. (C). The main subject *pulses* is plural, so the main verb must be plural. The correct answer is *light are*. (Note that *light* belongs to the previous prepositional phrase and is not connected to the verb, even though it looks so.)
31. (D). The wrong preposition is used. The correct answer is *the coast of*.
32. (C). The wrong clause marker is used. The correct answer is *where changes*.
33. (A). The preposition *to* is inappropriate here and should be removed.
34. (C). The wrong verb/preposition combination is used. The correct answer is *believed in*.
35. (B). The choice of verb is inappropriate. The correct answer is *makes*.
36. (C). This is a problem of redundancy, since *pass into* means *enter*. (C) should be removed.
37. (A). *Equipment* is a noncountable noun, so it should not be plural. The correct answer is *laser equipment*.
38. (B). The choice of word is inappropriate. The correct answer is *general sense*.
39. (C). The choice of preposition is inappropriate. The correct answer is *over*.
40. (B). The action is finished in past time, so the verb should be past tense. The correct answer is *became*.

VOCABULARY AND READING COMPREHENSION

The third section of the TOEFL tests your knowledge of vocabulary and your reading ability. Both the short-form and long-form versions (described in the Preface) are composed of two parts:

Vocabulary (Part A)
Reading Comprehension (Part B)

For the short-form TOEFL, you have 45 minutes to complete the 60 questions in Section 3. You should spend about 10 minutes on Part A and 35 minutes on Part B.

For the long-form TOEFL, you have 65 minutes to complete the 90 questions in Section 3. You should spend about 20 minutes on Part A and 45 minutes on Part B.

NOTE: On the TOEFL exam, only Section 1 is formally divided into three parts (Part A, Part B, and Part C). For some reason, the two parts of Section 3 are not identified in this way. In this handbook, we will use "A" and "B" as a convenient way to refer to each part.

Vocabulary (Part A)

In Part A you read sentences that contain an underlined word or phrase. You have to choose the answer that is CLOSEST IN MEANING to the underlined word or phrase.

MODEL

The views of U.S. Democrats often <u>diverge</u> from those of Republicans, especially in the area of foreign affairs.

(A) derive
(B) differ
(C) analyze
(D) develop

The term *diverge* means *differ*. The correct answer is (B).

Part A requires strong knowledge of college-level vocabulary. Unfortunately, you cannot develop this knowledge quickly; it comes with much time and study. One good approach is to make lists or flashcards of vocabulary and to review the words regularly. Additional information on using this approach can be found in Appendix C (page 153).

Part A can also include idiomatic expressions, especially verbal forms. If you haven't already done so, you should study the idioms in Appendix A (page 133) very carefully.

Word Analysis

One way to find the meaning of an unknown word is through ANALYSIS OF ITS PARTS. Prefixes and stems can sometimes help you to analyze words you don't know.

- A PREFIX is a form added before a word to change its meaning.

    1. It has long been considered <u>infeasible</u> to produce superconductors that operate at room temperatures.

        (A) attainable
        (B) desirable
        (C) impractical
        (D) impenetrable

        The word *infeasible* begins with the prefix *in-*, meaning "not." Answers (C) and (D) contain the prefix *im-*, which also means "not." These are the only possible choices. (C) is the correct answer.

- A STEM is the main part of a word to which other forms can be added.

    2. The lungs are the chief organs of <u>respiration</u> in human beings and other animals.

        (A) oxygen
        (B) creation
        (C) breathing
        (D) activity

        The Latin stem *-spir-* means "breathe." Prefixes can be added to the stem to form words such as *respire* and *inspire*. Suffixes (attached to the ends of stems) can be added to form words such as *respiration* and *inspiring*. (C) is the correct answer.

- A prefix can be added to a stem to form a new word.

    3. The U.S. Government stockpiles petroleum reserves in strategically located <u>subterranean</u> caves.

        (A) enormous
        (B) underground
        (C) protected
        (D) secretive

        Sub- is a prefix that means "under"; *-terra-* is a stem that means "earth." (B) is the correct answer.

- The following common prefixes are organized into groups having the same meaning.

NOT	a-	atypical
	un-	unusual
	dis-	disappear
	in-	incredible
	im-	impossible
	il-	illegal
	ir-	irresponsible
AGAIN	re-	reconsider

BACK	retro-		retroactive
BEFORE	ante- pre-		antecedent predict
TOGETHER	co- syn-		cooperate synonym
MANY	multi- poly-		multicolored polygon

- A list of the most common prefixes and stems can be found in Appendix C (page 153). You should be sure to review them carefully.

- Suffixes (attached to the ends of stems) are not important in Part A because all of the answer choices in a question will have the same grammatical form. In the first example above, the answer choices are all adjectives; in the second example, the answer choices are all nouns. Suffixes are used only to change one grammatical form to another, so they are not important in Part A.

Context Clues

Sometimes you can determine the meaning of a word from its CONTEXT. The term *context* refers to the meanings of other words in a sentence, as well as the overall meaning of the sentence.

- Pieces of information that help you to determine the meaning of unknown vocabulary are called CONTEXT CLUES.

    4. Prehistoric man farmed the land by using <u>primitive</u> tools fashioned with rock and wood.

    (A) advanced
    (B) metallic
    (C) simple
    (D) decorative

    The term *prehistoric* tells you that the time is in the distant past. The terms *rock and wood* suggest that the tools were made by hand of available material. These context clues indicate that the correct answer is (C).

- Generally, you should use context clues in three situations:
    a. You have some idea of the meaning of the underlined word, but you aren't sure. In this case, the context could help you to decide.
    b. You know what the underlined word means, but you aren't sure which answer is correct. In this case, you use context to eliminate the impossible answers and then guess from the remaining choices.
    c. You notice that the underlined word has more than one possible meaning. You should check the context to see which meaning is being used and then choose the appropriate answer.

- You have to be careful in using context because sometimes it could lead you to choose the wrong answer.

5. The Watergate burglary was a <u>bungled</u> attempt to influence the outcome of the 1972 Presidential elections.

    (A) political
    (B) illegal
    (C) inefficient
    (D) decisive

The word *burglary* suggests that the answer might be (B). The term *elections* suggests that the answer might be (A). However, neither of these choices means the same as *bungled*. The correct answer is (C).

Strategies for Part A

- Once again, you should not read the directions for Part A. Start working on the questions right away.

- You should look at an underlined word WITHOUT reading the sentence first. If you are certain you know the word, choose the answer that is closest in meaning (the synonym). If you have never seen the word before, check for prefixes or stems that may give you an idea of the meaning. If there are none, then guess at an answer and move on to the next question.

- In some cases you have seen the word before but you can't remember its exact meaning. First look for any prefixes or stems; then read the sentence quickly to locate possible context clues.

- In other cases you know the underlined word, but you cannot decide on the correct answer choice. First read the sentence quickly for context clues. If possible, use these context clues to eliminate impossible answers. Finally, guess from the remaining answers.

- The vocabulary becomes very difficult halfway through Part A. You will probably have to guess at most of the remaining answers. You can't afford to spend time trying to figure out the meaning of unknown words. You have to KEEP GOING, or you may be unable to finish Part B.

- Some students like to start with Part B, leaving Part A for the end. This is one way to allow enough time to complete all the reading passages. If you decide to use this approach, you must remember to start with the right number when you mark your answers on the answer sheet.

Vocabulary Practice

This exercise provides practice using the strategies for Part A you have just learned. Try to complete the exercise within 10 minutes.

<u>Directions:</u> In questions 1–30, each sentence has a word or phrase underlined. Below each sentence are four choices, and you must select the one that MOST CLOSELY MEANS THE SAME AS the underlined word.

Example

Meteorologists use balloons to <u>forecast</u> weather patterns.

(A) cause
(B) predict
(C) create
(D) test

(B) is the correct answer because the word "predict" most closely means "forecast."

Now begin work on the questions.

1. In the Middle Ages, minstrels were singing poets who <u>journeyed</u> throughout Europe earning their living.

   (A) worked
   (B) travelled
   (C) resided
   (D) associated

2. The Universal Product Code was <u>first</u> introduced in 1973 and is now used extensively in the manufacturing and retail industries.

   (A) initially
   (B) primarily
   (C) probably
   (D) orderly

3. The Great Depression of 1933 occurred because banks lent money to people who could not <u>pay back</u> their loans.

   (A) refinance
   (B) purchase
   (C) return
   (D) negotiate

4. The technique of putting colorful designs on <u>fabric</u> is called batik.

   (A) metal
   (B) plastic
   (C) rubber
   (D) cloth

GO ON TO THE NEXT PAGE ➤

5. Ludwig van Beethoven was one of the <u>great</u> composers in the history of music.

   (A) outstanding
   (B) large
   (C) reliable
   (D) deliberate

6. A <u>pole</u> with red and white spiral stripes is still the symbol of a barber's shop.

   (A) rectangle
   (B) stick
   (C) wire
   (D) figure

7. Most bears spend the better part of the winter in a continual <u>state</u> of hibernation.

   (A) country
   (B) perception
   (C) condition
   (D) danger

8. In basketball, a jump shot is made at the <u>apex</u> of a player's leap in the air.

   (A) onset
   (B) perimeter
   (C) edge
   (D) peak

9. Forty-six microscopic structures called chromosomes form the <u>foundation</u> of individual growth and development.

   (A) basis
   (B) discovery
   (C) experimentation
   (D) concentration

10. Bedouins are very <u>spirited</u> and independent people who live in the deserts of the Middle East.

    (A) delightful
    (B) proud
    (C) disrespectful
    (D) quiet

11. The <u>derivation</u> of the term "bank" is from the Italian word "banca," meaning "bench."

    (A) origin
    (B) reference
    (C) distinction
    (D) similarity

12. Although the Red Cross is <u>widely</u> known for its work during wartime, it also aids people during natural disasters.

    (A) specifically
    (B) generally
    (C) occasionally
    (D) spaciously

13. Many people use barbiturates to relieve tension and often suffer withdrawal symptoms when trying to <u>give up</u> their dependence.

    (A) rehabilitate
    (B) modify
    (C) decrease
    (D) terminate

14. The two <u>stages</u> preceding the birth of a child are the embryo (during the first two months) and the fetus (during the last seven months).

    (A) platforms
    (B) types
    (C) scenes
    (D) steps

GO ON TO THE NEXT PAGE ➤

15. Lionel Barrymore was <u>a celebrated</u> actor in the theater, radio, and movies, as well as a musician and composer.

    (A) an acclaimed
    (B) an industrious
    (C) a talented
    (D) an inscrutable

16. Pollination <u>transpires</u> when insects such as bees carry pollen on their feet from one flower to another.

    (A) develops
    (B) occurs
    (C) transfers
    (D) fertilizes

17. Bacteria can be both <u>detrimental</u> and helpful to humans, depending on the specific type and effect.

    (A) productive
    (B) useful
    (C) harmful
    (D) fatal

18. Automatic teller machines are a <u>very</u> convenient means of obtaining cash 24 hours a day.

    (A) extremely
    (B) somewhat
    (C) more
    (D) considerably

19. Prostitution is <u>an illicit</u> activity in all states except Nevada.

    (A) an unlawful
    (B) a disgusting
    (C) a familiar
    (D) an irresponsible

20. A barometer is <u>a device</u> for measuring changes in atmospheric pressure.

    (A) a method
    (B) an invention
    (C) a figure
    (D) an instrument

21. If properly worn and <u>secured</u>, safety belts could save between 12,000 and 15,000 lives each year.

    (A) manufactured
    (B) released
    (C) attached
    (D) designed

22. Alcoholism is the third leading cause of death and <u>afflicts</u> over 10 million Americans annually.

    (A) rejuvenates
    (B) controls
    (C) destroys
    (D) affects

23. <u>Inadequate</u> supply of oxygen to the blood can cause death within minutes.

    (A) Abundant
    (B) Insufficient
    (C) Substantial
    (D) Nonexistent

24. It is generally <u>recognized</u> that Asia was the cradle of civilization about 5,500 years ago.

    (A) known
    (B) determined
    (C) challenged
    (D) distributed

GO ON TO THE NEXT PAGE ▶

83

25. Animals were first <u>domesticated</u> as a source of food and later as a source of clothing and transportation.

(A) raised
(B) bought
(C) found
(D) tamed

26. Great art is characterized by its ability to <u>invigorate</u> the senses with its power.

(A) absorb
(B) control
(C) refresh
(D) expand

27. Postmodernism is a prominent yet <u>controversial</u> movement in the field of architecture.

(A) unanimous
(B) disputable
(C) ancient
(D) unique

28. One of the earliest pioneers in the field of aerodynamics was Leonardo da Vinci, who is better recognized for his artistic <u>achievements</u>.

(A) attitudes
(B) accomplishments
(C) habits
(D) masterpieces

29. Circuses in the early 1900s were <u>notorious</u> for using humans who had freak body characteristics.

(A) enjoyable
(B) infamous
(C) illegal
(D) discriminatory

30. The Barbizon school of French painters was well known for landscapes that captured the <u>subtle</u> beauty of scenery through gentle lighting and soft colors.

(A) obvious
(B) delightful
(C) receding
(D) elusive

Explanations and Answers begin on the following page.

Explanations and Answers for Vocabulary Practice

1. (B).
2. (A).
3. (C). *Pay back* is an idiomatic expression.
4. (D).
5. (A). *Great* can also mean *large* (B), but the context does not support this answer.
6. (B).
7. (C). *State* can also mean *country* (A), but the context does not support this answer.
8. (D). The context suggest the top, or *peak*, of a jump.
9. (A).
10. (B).
11. (A).
12. (B). Something that is wide is also spacious (D), but the context does not support this answer.
13. (D). *Give up* is an idiomatic expression.
14. (D).
15. (A).
16. (B).
17. (C).
18. (A).
19. (A). The prefix *il-* means "not." Both (A) and (D) have prefixes with the same meaning, which limits your choice.
20. (D).
21. (C).
22. (D).
23. (B). The prefix *in-* means "not." Both (B) and (D) have prefixes with the same meaning, limiting your choice.
24. (A).
25. (D). The context suggests that (A) and (B) are possible, but only (D) is a true synonym.
26. (C). *In-* is a prefix meaning "into." It does not have a negative meaning as in 23.
27. (B).
28. (B).
29. (B).
30. (D).

Reading Comprehension (Part B)

Part B tests your understanding of concepts and vocabulary in academic reading passages. You have to choose the BEST ANSWER to each question about a passage.

MODEL

       For most people, the distinction between vegetables and fruits is fairly clear. Scientists, however, have varied opinions in this regard. For example, horticulturists categorize a watermelon as a vegetable despite its general acceptance as a fruit. Botanists identify a tomato as a fruit even though it is commonly used as a vegetable.

(5)   These differences stem from the ways in which fruits and vegetables are classified. For a botanist, a fruit is the seed-bearing portion of a flowering plant or tree. According to this definition, a tomato is a fruit. For a horticulturist, a vegetable is the edible portion of a plant that must be replanted annually. According to this view, a tomato is a vegetable. A horticulturist sees a fruit as coming from a plant or tree that

(10)   lives at least two years. In the case of fruits and vegetables that meet the criteria of both groups of scientists, such as apples or potatoes, there is no conflict.

The following SAMPLE QUESTIONS are used in this section to discuss the kinds of questions that occur in Part B. Try to answer the questions at this time.

1. What does this passage mainly discuss?

   (A) The work of botanists and horticulturists
   (B) Common types of fruits and vegetables
   (C) Scientific differences between fruits and vegetables
   (D) The seed-bearing nature of fruit

2. According to the passage, the scientific classification of a watermelon by horticulturists

   (A) differs from its popular description as a fruit
   (B) remains a major area of disagreement between scientists
   (C) places it within the categories of both fruit and vegetable
   (D) is no longer open to debate among members of the scientific community

3. In line 4, the pronoun "it" refers to

   (A) a fruit
   (B) a vegetable
   (C) a watermelon
   (D) a tomato

4. In the last line, the word "conflict" could best be replaced by which of the following?

   (A) Consensus
   (B) Disagreement
   (C) Classification
   (D) Solution

5. Which of the following conclusions about fruits can be drawn from the passage?

   (A) Some fruits are not edible.
   (B) Fruits develop from the flowers of plants and trees.
   (C) Some fruits do not develop seeds.
   (D) Botanists have studied fruits more carefully than horticulturists have.

Reading for the Main Idea

One type of question in Part B involves identifying the MAIN IDEA of a passage.

- A main idea question asks you to identify what a passage is about IN GENERAL. It should accurately describe the overall purpose of most of the sentences in a passage.

- The correct answer for a main idea question cannot be too general. It should not include ideas that are beyond the topic of the passage.

- The correct answer for a main idea question cannot be too specific. It cannot be limited to particular details, reasons, or examples given in the passage.

- Question 1 is a MAIN IDEA question.

1. What does the passage mainly discuss?

    (A) The work of botanists and horticulturists
    (B) Common types of fruits and vegetables
    (C) Scientific differences between fruits and vegetables
    (D) The seed-bearing nature of fruit

Answers (A) and (B) are too general. (A) is wrong because the opinions could include areas not covered in this passage. (B) is wrong because a discussion of types of fruits and vegetables is beyond the topic of this passage.

Answer (D) is too specific. It is mentioned in line 6 as an example of one difference in classification. The example supports the main idea of the passage.

(C) is the correct answer. It accurately describes the overall purpose of the passage.

- The main idea of a passage can usually be found by reading the first sentence of each paragraph in the passage. The first sentence of the second paragraph in the model clearly indicates the main idea:

    "These differences stem from the ways in which fruits and vegetables are classified."

Sometimes the first sentence of a passage is a general introduction to the topic. In this case, the main idea can usually be found in the second sentence of the passage. This situation is illustrated by the first two sentences of the sample passage:

"For most people, the distinction between vegetables and fruits is fairly clear." (general introduction)
"Scientists, however, have varied opinions in this regard." (main idea follows the introduction)

Because of this fact, it is advisable to read the first TWO sentences of the first paragraph and the first sentence of all subsequent paragraphs when trying to determine the main idea of a passage.

- The following questions may be used to ask for the MAIN IDEA:

"What is the main topic of this passage?"
"What does the passage mainly discuss?"
"What is the author's main point?"
"The main theme of the passage is..."
"Which of the following is the best title for the passage?"

All the questions above contain the word *main* except the last one. The best title for a passage should accurately reflect the main idea.

- If there is a main idea question for a passage, it is usually the first question. Most passages start with a main idea question.

Reading for Details

Another type of question in Part B involves identifying a specific DETAIL in the passage.

- Details are FACTS that are clearly stated in a passage. To answer a question, you have to locate the appropriate fact.

- In most cases, a detail question requires you to choose the answer that is a PARAPHRASE of some fact in a passage. A paraphrase provides the same meaning but differs somewhat in vocabulary and grammar.

- Question 2 is a DETAIL question.

    2. According to the passage, the scientific classification of a watermelon by horticulturists

    (A) diverges from its popular description as a fruit
    (B) remains a major area of disagreement between scientists
    (C) places it within the categories of both fruit and vegetable
    (D) is no longer open to debate among members of the scientific community

    The correct answer is located in lines 2 and 3 of the passage. These lines indicate that horticulturists classify a watermelon as a vegetable, even though it is generally accepted as a fruit. You have to find the answer that most closely has the same meaning.

    (A) is the correct answer. It is a suitable paraphrase of the information in the passage. The other answer choices are not factually correct according to the passage.

- The following forms may be used to introduce DETAIL questions:

    ''According to the passage . . .''
    ''The passage states that . . .''
    ''The author states that . . .''
    ''What does the author say about . . .''
    ''All of the following are mentioned EXCEPT . . .''
    ''Which of the following is NOT supported by . . .''

- The last two forms above are the most difficult because they involve finding the one WRONG answer. To do this, first you have to find the three answers that ARE mentioned in the passage; the remaining answer is the one not mentioned. This kind of question often takes too much of your time.

- Question 3 is a special type of detail question involving PRONOUN REFERENCE.

    3. In line 4, the pronoun ''it'' refers to

    (A) a fruit
    (B) a vegetable
    (C) a watermelon
    (D) a tomato

    A tomato is commonly used as a vegetable, so *it* refers to a tomato. (D) is the correct answer. The other choices do not make any sense in this context.

- Question 4 is a special type of detail question involving VOCABULARY.

    4. In the last line, the word ''conflict'' could best be replaced by which of the following?

    (A) Consensus
    (B) Disagreement
    (C) Classification
    (D) Solution

    (B) is the correct answer. *Disagreement* is a synonym of *conflict*. The context in the last sentence tells you that scientists agree on the classification of many fruits and vegetables (''that meet the criteria of both groups''). In many cases there is no conflict, meaning there is no disagreement.

Reading for Inferences

Another type of question in Part B involves making an INFERENCE from the passage.

- An inference is a CONCLUSION that can be made from the details in a passage. The inference is not directly stated in the passage; it is suggested by one or more facts.

- Question 5 is an INFERENCE question.

    5. Which of the following conclusions about fruits can be drawn from the passage?

        (A) Some fruits are not edible.
        (B) Fruits develop from the flowers of plants and trees.
        (C) Some fruits do not develop seeds.
        (D) Botanists have studied fruits more carefully than horticulturists have.

    Line 6 indicates that fruit is the seed-bearing portion of a flowering plant or tree. You can conclude that flowers are needed in order for fruit to develop. (B) is the correct answer. The passage doesn't state this idea directly, but you can understand it from the facts.

- Inference questions can be the hardest type of question on the TOEFL. You really have to think carefully to decide on the correct answer. It is very easy to spend too much time on inference questions.

- The following forms may be used to introduce inference questions:

    "It can be inferred from the passage that..."
    "The author implies that..."
    "The passage suggests that..."
    "It is possible that..."
    "It is likely that..."
    "The passage supports which of the following conclusions?"

- One special kind of inference question requires you to decide what ADDITIONAL passage might precede or follow a given passage. Typical questions might be:

    "The previous paragraph most likely discusses..."
    "The paragraph following the passage most probably discusses..."

    In the case of the sample passage, the following paragraph might discuss areas of agreement between horticulturists and botanists.

- Another special kind of inference question requires you to decide on the SOURCE of a passage. A typical question might be:

    "The passage would most likely be found in a textbook on which of the following subjects?"

    In the case of the sample passage, the source might be a book on agriculture.

Strategies for Part B

It is again unnecessary to read the directions. Start working on the passages immediately.

- Do the passages in order from the beginning. The passages and questions generally increase in difficulty.

- When you start a passage, read the first TWO sentences of the first paragraph and the first sentence of the rest of the paragraphs to learn the purpose of the passage. Do not read the other parts of the passage at this time.

- Spend about one minute answering each question. You should follow these steps:

  1. Identify any important words in a question (called KEY TERMS) that would help you to locate the answer in the passage. Also note the type of question (main idea, detail, inference).
  2. Try to find the answer in the passage by looking for the KEY TERMS from the question or for words having the same meaning as the key terms. Remember that the correct answer is often a paraphrase of information in the passage.
  3. Return to the question and choose the correct answer. If you are somewhat uncertain, go back to the reading to check again. If you still cannot determine the correct answer, eliminate the impossible answers and then guess.

The following are two general observations about Part B:

- The correct answers can be found through a passage in approximately the same order as the questions. The answers to one or two questions may be out of order, but most will be in order. This is the main reason why you don't have to read the entire passage before answering the questions.

- Do not waste time trying to find answers to difficult questions. After a minute or so, guess and move on to the next question. You can put a small mark next to a question on your answer sheet (NOT in your test booklet) if you want to go back to it later. Be sure to erase any such marks before the end of the time period.

Reading Practice

This exercise provides practice using the strategies for Part B you have just learned. Try to complete the exercise within 35 minutes.

Directions: In this part you will read passages on various topics and answer questions about them. Some answers to the questions are directly stated, while others are only suggested.

Read the following passage:

The pituitary gland, one of the body's key organs, generates a number of hormones that help control body function. Sometimes known as the hypophysis, the gland has two main parts—the anterior lobe and the posterior lobe. It is about the size of a pea and is located near the center of the skull.

Example I

According to the passage, what is another name for the pituitary gland?

(A) The anterior lobe
(B) The hormone
(C) The hypophysis
(D) The posterior lobe

The passage states that the pituitary gland is also known as the hypophysis. Therefore, the correct answer is (C).

Example II

It can be inferred from the passage that the pituitary gland is

(A) quite small
(B) divided into several parts
(C) very large
(D) composed of a number of hormones

The passage states that the pituitary gland is about the size of a pea, which suggests that it is quite small. The correct answer is (A).

Now begin work on the questions.

GO ON TO THE NEXT PAGE

Questions 1–6

People commonly complain that they never have enough time to accomplish tasks. The hours and minutes seem to slip away before many planned chores get done. According to time management experts, the main reason for this is that most people fail to set priorities about what to do

(5) first. They get tied down by trivial, time-consuming matters and never complete the important ones.

One simple solution often used by those at the top is to keep lists of tasks to be accomplished daily. These lists order jobs from most essential to least essential and are checked regularly through the day to assess progress.

(10) Not only is this an effective way to manage time, but also it serves to give individuals a much-deserved sense of satisfaction over their achievements. People who do not keep lists often face the end of the work day with uncertainty over the significance of their accomplishments, which over time can contribute to serious problems in mental and physical health.

1. Which of the following is the best title for the passage?

(A) Common Complaints About Work
(B) Accomplishing Trivial Matters
(C) Achieving Job Satisfaction
(D) Learning to Manage Time

2. According to the passage, why do many people never seem to have enough time to accomplish things?

(A) They do not prioritize tasks.
(B) They get tied down by one difficult problem.
(C) They fail to deal with trivial matters.
(D) They do not seek the advice of time management experts.

3. In line 7, the word "those" refers to

(A) daily lists
(B) trivial matters
(C) priorities
(D) people

4. The passage states that one solution to time management problems is to

(A) consult a time management expert
(B) accomplish time-consuming matters first
(C) keep daily lists of priorities and check them regularly
(D) spend only a short time on each task

5. In line 11, the word "achievements" could best be replaced by which of the following?

(A) Assessments
(B) Priorities
(C) Decisions
(D) Accomplishments

6. The paragraph following the passage most probably discusses

(A) mental and physical health problems
(B) another solution to time management problems
(C) ways to achieve a sense of fulfillment
(D) different types of lists

GO ON TO THE NEXT PAGE ➤

Questions 7–12

A professor of anthropology at the University of Tucson has created an entirely new field of science called garbology. William Rathje and his students have been studying the garbage left for collection in front of Tucson homes since 1973. With the help of the local sanitation company,

(5) they have inspected and categorized some 120 tons of garbage and have arrived at some interesting conclusions.

One result is that middle-income families waste more food than lower- or upper-income families. Another fact is that poor families pay more for their food and household items than wealthy families because they cannot

(10) afford to buy it in bulk. Finally, the overall waste figure is down to 15 percent, about half the figure from the first quarter of this century. This can be attributed to modern methods of refrigeration, transportation, processing, and packaging.

7. What does the passage mainly discuss?

(A) The creation of a new science
(B) The job of an anthropology professor
(C) Results from work in the field of garbology
(D) Methods of handling food products

8. According to the passage, who is William Rathje?

(A) A sanitation engineer
(B) A university student
(C) A government scientist
(D) An anthropology professor

9. What did William Rathje and his students examine?

(A) A local sanitation company
(B) The fronts of homes in Tucson, Arizona
(C) Garbage left on streets for collection
(D) Modern methods of refrigeration

10. It can be inferred from the passage that the science of garbology is important because it

(A) offers work opportunities for university students
(B) provides insights into the lifestyles of American families
(C) is the newest science to be developed
(D) is a cooperative venture of the university and the local sanitation company

GO ON TO THE NEXT PAGE

11. Which of the following is NOT mentioned as a reason for the decrease in waste since the first quarter of this century?

(A) Better eating habits of Americans
(B) Improved methods of refrigerating food
(C) Faster means of transporting perishable foods
(D) Superior methods of packaging products

12. According to the passage, why do the poor pay more for their food than the rich?

(A) They are more careless with their money.
(B) They are unable to purchase large quantities at a time.
(C) They shop at more expensive stores.
(D) They do not earn as much money.

GO ON TO THE NEXT PAGE

Questions 13–20

Many countries face a somewhat more serious economic problem in the form of an unfavorable trade balance with other nations. Such an imbalance exists when the total value of a country's imports exceeds that of its exports. For example, if a country buys $25 billion in products from
(5)   other countries, yet sells only $10 billion of its own products overseas, its trade deficit is $15 billion. Many underdeveloped nations find themselves in this position because they lack natural resources or the industrial capacity to use these resources, and thus have to import raw materials or manufactured goods.
(10)   One effect of a trade deficit is the flow of currency out of a country. In the case of an underdeveloped nation, this can cause many financial difficulties, including failure to meet debt payments and obstacles to creation of an industrial base. Even in the case of a fully developed nation such as the United States, a large trade deficit is reason for alarm. American
(15)   products, made by well-paid workers in U.S. industries, cost more to produce than those made in places like Asia, where labor and material costs are much lower. Money spent on foreign products is money not spent on items produced by domestic industries.

13. What does the passage mainly discuss?

(A) Several worldwide economic problems
(B) The causes and consequences of trade deficits
(C) Lack of resources in underdeveloped countries
(D) The value of exports versus imports

14. According to the passage, when does a trade imbalance occur?

(A) A country has a serious economic problem.
(B) A country sells more products overseas than it imports.
(C) The value of the products a country imports is greater than the value of the products it exports.
(D) A country cannot develop its natural resources.

15. In line 6, the word "deficit" could best be replaced by which of the following?

(A) Shortage
(B) Situation
(C) Increase
(D) Products

16. The passage states that many underdeveloped nations have trade deficits because

(A) they find themselves in this position
(B) they export most of their natural resources to other nations
(C) they have to import most of their natural resources or manufactured products
(D) they have failed to meet debt payments

GO ON TO THE NEXT PAGE

17. The paragraph preceding the passage most probably discusses

    (A) countries with favorable trade balances
    (B) a less serious economic problem faced by many nations
    (C) various types of export and import items
    (D) other effects of a trade imbalance

18. In line 16, "those" refers to

    (A) industries
    (B) workers
    (C) products
    (D) trade deficits

19. Which of the following is NOT mentioned as a possible cause of a trade imbalance?

    (A) Low labor and material costs in Asian countries
    (B) A lack of natural resources
    (C) An undeveloped industrial base
    (D) The high cost of exported items

20. It can be inferred from this passage that American industries

    (A) do not pay their workers sufficient wages
    (B) are hurt by a trade imbalance
    (C) import labor and material from overseas
    (D) provide a strong industrial base that prevents a trade deficit

GO ON TO THE NEXT PAGE

97

Questions 21–25

Hundreds of thousands of persons each year fall prey to some type of cancer, but new methods of radiation therapy have enabled doctors to save more lives than ever before. Medical researchers have developed several experimental forms of this time-honored cancer treatment that seem
(5) effective in fighting the disease.

One promising approach involves exposing cancer cells to radiation by implanting a radioactive source directly into the malignant tissue. This process greatly increases the dosage and thus the effectiveness of the treatment. Another technique utilizes drugs to make cancer cells more
(10) susceptible to the effects of radiation and to make normal cells more resistant. Certain drugs are able to neutralize the genetic framework of cancer cells, thus making them more easily affected by radiation. Both techniques have seen some positive results in the treatment of inoperable brain tumors.

(15) These and other methods have helped to raise the recovery rate for cancer victims from 30 percent 40 years ago to around 50 percent today. This is encouraging news for those who fall prey to one of the world's leading killers.

21. What is the author's main purpose in the passage?

   (A) To provide statistical information on cancer
   (B) To argue for new methods of cancer treatment
   (C) To illustrate new techniques of radiation therapy
   (D) To give the results of recent cancer research

22. According to the passage, which of the following is true about radiation therapy?

   (A) There is only one effective form of this therapy.
   (B) It saves millions of lives each year.
   (C) It is an accepted method of cancer treatment.
   (D) It causes the incidence of cancer to rise dramatically.

23. In line 7, the word "malignant" most closely means

   (A) diseased
   (B) experimental
   (C) treated
   (D) porous

GO ON TO THE NEXT PAGE

24. According to the passage, radiation therapy is most effective when

   (A) drugs are used to relax the cancer patient
   (B) the cancer is directly exposed to the radioactive material
   (C) it is used on as many patients as possible
   (D) the cancer cells are resistant to treatment

25. It can be inferred from the passage that

   (A) improvements in cancer treatment during the last half century have been relatively ineffective
   (B) the number of deaths caused by cancer has decreased substantially
   (C) fewer people are susceptible to the effects of cancer
   (D) scientists are close to eliminating cancer entirely

GO ON TO THE NEXT PAGE

Questions 26–30

Other American authors have written about the struggle of the rural poor to overcome economic and social obstacles, but none have done so with more authority than John Steinbeck, winner of the 1962 Nobel Prize for literature. Steinbeck achieved fame for his moving portrayals of the
(5)   oppressed farm laborers in and around his hometown of Salinas, California. His vivid descriptions of the lives of migrant workers and poor farmers in his first novel, *Tortilla Flat* (1935), attracted the attention of critics and the reading public, launching a long and productive career.

Steinbeck continued to deal with the battle against social adversity in
(10)   two subsequent novels, *Of Mice and Men* (1937) and *The Grapes of Wrath* (1939). The latter is his most illustrious work, earning him the 1940 Pulitzer Prize. In it Steinbeck told the story of a poor Oklahoma family that migrated to California during the Great Depression of the 1930s in order to start a new life. Steinbeck related with sympathy and understanding how
(15)   this family faced discrimination and mistreatment at the hands of police and employers. The novel was acclaimed as a masterful portrayal of the search for human dignity.

Steinbeck was a prolific writer for the next two decades, but most critics did not receive his work with the same praise they gave his fiction of
(20)   the 1930s. Two of his better-known novels were *The Winter of Our Discontent* (1961) and *Travels with Charlie* (1962), an entertaining tale of a journey Steinbeck undertook with his pet poodle.

26. Which of the following is the best title for the passage?

(A) The Struggle of the Poor
(B) Famous American Authors
(C) The 1962 Nobel Prize Winner
(D) The Work of John Steinbeck

27. Which of the following conclusions about John Steinbeck is supported by the passage?

(A) His childhood exposure to the living conditions of the rural poor qualified him to describe their lives.
(B) He was the first author to win a Nobel Prize in literature for a work of fiction about oppressed people.
(C) He employed a unique style of composition that set new standards for future authors.
(D) He was the only writer whose first novel attracted so much attention from the critics and the reading public.

GO ON TO THE NEXT PAGE ▶

28. According to the passage, which novel was Steinbeck's most successful effort?

    (A) *Tortilla Flat* (1935)
    (B) *Of Mice and Men* (1937)
    (C) *The Grapes of Wrath* (1939)
    (D) *The Winter of Our Discontent* (1961)

29. According to the passage, Steinbeck's story of a poor Oklahoma migrant family was acclaimed as

    (A) a skillful description of the pursuit of dignity
    (B) a thorough account of life during the Great Depression
    (C) a major contribution towards reform in labor relations during the 1940s
    (D) an attempt to portray the rural poor as responsible for their own misfortune

30. It can be inferred from the passage that Steinbeck's novels after the 1930s

    (A) exceeded the standards set by his initial efforts
    (B) rarely achieved the same level of quality as his earlier work
    (C) continued to receive the critical acclaim of reviewers
    (D) earned him numerous literary and monetary awards

STOP   STOP   STOP   STOP   STOP   STOP   STOP

Explanations and Answers for Reading Practice

Questions 1–6

1. Type: Main Idea
   Key terms: best title
   Answer: (D)

   (D) accurately describes the overall purpose of the passage. (A) is too general; (B) and (C) are too specific.

2. Type: Detail
   Key terms: why, never have enough time
   Answer: (A)

   The answer can be found in lines 3–5. The key term *why* in the question indicates reason, which begins in line 4.

3. Type: Detail
   Key terms: line 7, those
   Answer: (D)

   The word *those* occurs in the context of using a solution and keeping lists, which are things only people can do.

4. Type: Detail
   Key terms: solution
   Answer: (C)

   The answer can be found in the second paragraph. The key term *solution* leads you to the answer starting in line 7.

5. Type: Detail
   Key terms: line 11, achievements, replaced by
   Answer: (D)

   The synonym for *achievements* can be found in line 13.

6. Type: Inference
   Key terms: paragraph following
   Answer: (B)

   The first sentence of the second paragraph introduces one solution. You can infer that the next paragraph will discuss another solution. (Note that the correct answer does not come from the last sentence of the second paragraph, where you might first think it would. This is an important fact to remember for this kind of question.)

Questions 7–12

7. Type: Main Idea
   Key terms: mainly discuss
   Answer: (C)

   (C) correctly identifies the overall purpose of the passage. (A) and (B) are too general; (D) is too specific.

8. Type: Detail
   Key terms: William Rathje
   Answer: (D)

William Rathje is identified in line 1 as a professor of anthropology.

9. Type: Detail
   Key terms: examine
   Answer: (C)

The answer is given in lines 2–4.

10. Type: Inference
    Key terms: garbology, important, because
    Answer: (B)

The second paragraph lists some interesting conclusions about American families. From these you can infer answer (B). The other answers are not good inferences from this context.

11. Type: Detail
    Key terms: NOT mentioned, reason, decrease in waste
    Answer: (A)

Answers (B), (C), and (D) are all mentioned in the last two lines of the second paragraph. This is an easy question because all the valid reasons are mentioned in order.

12. Type: Detail
    Key terms: poor, pay more
    Answer: (B)

The answer is in lines 9 and 10. *To buy in bulk* means *to purchase large quantities.*

Questions 13–20

13. Type: Main Idea
    Key terms: mainly discuss
    Answer: (B)

The second sentence of the first paragraph mentions a cause, while the first sentence of the second paragraph mentions a consequence, so (B) accurately describes the overall purpose of the passage. Answer (A) is too general. It might be the topic of an entire chapter of a book, not just two paragraphs. Answers (C) and (D) are too specific. They are details that support the main idea.

14. Type: Detail
    Key terms: when, trade imbalance
    Answer: (C)

The correct answer is found in the second sentence of the first paragraph (lines 2–4). The key term *when* leads you to this answer.

15. Type: Detail
    Key terms: line 6, deficit, replaced
    Answer: (A)

Shortage is a synonym of *deficit*. Lines 4–6 provide an example of a country that is short $15 billion in its trade balance. The other answers do not fit this context.

16. Type: Detail
Key terms: underdeveloped nations, deficits, because
Answer: (C)

The answer can be found in the last sentence of the first paragraph (lines 6–9). The key term *because* leads you to the answer starting in line 7.

17. Type: Inference
Key terms: paragraph preceding
Answer: (B)

The phrase *somewhat more serious economic problem* in line 1 suggests that the previous paragraph discussed a less serious problem.

18. Type: Detail
Key terms: line 16, those
Answer : (C)

The pronoun *those* refers back to the subject of the sentence in line 15.

19. Type: Detail
Key terms: NOT mentioned, cause, imbalance
Answer: (D)

(A) is mentioned in lines 16 and 17, while (B) and (C) are mentioned in lines 7 and 8. (C) is also mentioned in lines 12 and 13. (This is a very difficult question because the proper causes are mentioned in different parts of the passage. It may be best to guess at this kind of question quickly and move on.)

20. Type: Inference
Key terms: American industries
Answer: (B)

This is an inference that is suggested by the last two sentences of the second paragraph.

Questions 21–25

21. Type: Main Idea
Key terms: main purpose
Answer: (C)

The first paragraph talks about new methods of radiation therapy, and the second paragraph discusses two new techniques. Therefore, (C) best describes the overall purpose of the passage.

22. Type: Detail
Key terms: true, radiation therapy
Answer: (C)

(A), (B), and (D) are false according to the passage. The term *time-honored* in line 4 indicates the accepted nature of radiation therapy.

23. Type: Detail
Key terms: line 7, malignant
Answer: (A)

The word *malignant* means *diseased*. The context tells you that malignant tissue contains cancer cells, which cause the disease.

24. Type: Detail
    Key terms: radiation, effective when
    Answer: (B)

    The effectiveness of exposing cancer cells directly to radiation is mentioned in lines 6 and 7.

25. Type: Inference
    Key terms: (none)
    Answer: (B)

    The last paragraph indicates that the recovery rate has risen from 30 percent 40 years ago to 50 percent today. From this you understand that the number of deaths has decreased substantially.

Questions 26–30

26. Type: Main Idea
    Key terms: best title
    Answer: (D)

    (D) accurately describes the overall purpose of the passage. (A) and (B) are too general and are part of the introduction in the first part of the first sentence. (C) is too specific.

27. Type: Inference
    Key terms: John Steinbeck
    Answer: (A)

    In lines 2 and 3 you are told that Steinbeck has more authority to write about the rural poor than other writers, and in lines 4*6 you are told that Steinbeck grew up among farm laborers. From this information you can infer that (A) is correct.

28. Type: Detail
    Key terms: novel, most successful
    Answer: (C)

    Line 11 indicates that *The Grapes of Wrath* was Steinbeck's most illustrious work.

29. Type: Detail
    Key terms: Oklahoma migrant family, hailed
    Answer: (A)

    The answer is found in lines 16 and 17. The phrases *search for human dignity* and *pursuit of dignity* are synonymous.

30. Type: Inference
    Key terms: novels after the 1930s
    Answer: (B)

    The answer is suggested in lines 19 and 20. Critics would have praised his later works if they had been of the same quality as his earlier efforts.

Reading Practice Test

SECTION 3
VOCABULARY AND READING COMPREHENSION

Time—45 minutes

This section tests your understanding of written English. It is divided into two parts.

<u>Directions:</u> In questions 1–30 each sentence has a word or phrase underlined. Below each sentence are four choices, and you must select the one that MOST CLOSELY MEANS THE SAME AS the underlined word.

Example

Meteorologists use balloons to <u>forecast</u> weather patterns.

(A) cause
(B) predict
(C) create
(D) test

(B) is the correct answer because the word "predict" most closely means "forecast."

1. Unlike most birds, the brown thrasher does not <u>tolerate</u> nests of other birds near its own.

(A) build
(B) permit
(C) destroy
(D) inhabit

2. Public service <u>announcements</u> on radio and television are provided free of charge to qualifying agencies.

(A) deliveries
(B) advertisers
(C) statements
(D) regulations

3. Scientists have not yet determined the <u>precise</u> origins of the universe.

(A) previous
(B) unknown
(C) deceiving
(D) exact

4. The rise in deadly <u>communicable</u> diseases is of increasing concern among health professionals.

(A) metabolic
(B) culpable
(C) reflective
(D) transmittable

GO ON TO THE NEXT PAGE

5. Calligraphy is the art of drawing <u>elegant</u> characters by hand using a special pen.

   (A) obscure
   (B) rough
   (C) graceful
   (D) unusual

6. The squirrel is one of nature's wild creatures that has adapted well to a suburban <u>setting</u>.

   (A) scenery
   (B) establishment
   (C) environment
   (D) dwelling

7. Congressional subcommittees have the <u>right</u> to prevent legislation from reaching the floor for debate.

   (A) measure
   (B) authority
   (C) compromise
   (D) validity

8. John F. Kennedy, the first U.S. president born in the twentieth century, <u>captured</u> the imagination of the American people.

   (A) seized
   (B) characterized
   (C) instituted
   (D) described

9. Julius Caesar was trained as a politician <u>yet</u> quickly established a reputation as an ingenious military strategist.

   (A) until
   (B) even
   (C) but
   (D) except

10. The <u>principal</u> purpose of a labor union is to increase wages and benefits for its members.

    (A) registered
    (B) necessary
    (C) stated
    (D) chief

11. The Hague is the seat of the International Court of Justice, which mediates international political <u>discord</u>.

    (A) representation
    (B) conflict
    (C) election
    (D) arbitration

12. Calypso is a form of Caribbean folk music best known for cleverly worded phrases that <u>make up</u> the lyrics.

    (A) comprise
    (B) oversee
    (C) accompany
    (D) complement

13. Some individuals experience <u>a particular</u> allergic reaction to dairy products such as milk.

    (A) a distinct
    (B) a separate
    (C) a homogenized
    (D) an unpleasant

14. A labyrinth is a confusing and <u>seemingly</u> endless array of passages.

    (A) unlikely
    (B) apparently
    (C) continuously
    (D) deliberately

GO ON TO THE NEXT PAGE

15. Television and newspapers are the primary <u>mediums</u> of advertising, with radio a rapidly fading competitor.

    (A) formulations
    (B) averages
    (C) sources
    (D) means

16. Paper money is <u>an accepted</u> form of legal tender for all financial transactions except payment of custom duties and interest on the public debt.

    (A) a standard
    (B) an innovative
    (C) an intricate
    (D) a statistical

17. Royal families of Europe in the nineteenth century <u>maintained</u> power by arranging marriages with other royal families.

    (A) regulated
    (B) created
    (C) sustained
    (D) distributed

18. The camel, an animal of practical use to the desert people of Africa and Asia, has a highly <u>unpredictable</u> nature.

    (A) erratic
    (B) responsible
    (C) economical
    (D) pleasurable

19. The African continent is a vast, <u>latent</u> source of mineral wealth and hydroelectric power.

    (A) conducive
    (B) powerful
    (C) incomplete
    (D) potential

20. Light can be amplified and <u>focused</u> in a single direction by using a device called a laser.

    (A) concentrated
    (B) adjusted
    (C) clarified
    (D) scattered

21. The laws of nature determine that some animals will <u>nurture</u> their young from birth while others will leave offspring to survive on their own.

    (A) convalesce
    (B) shelter
    (C) nourish
    (D) predispose

22. The banana is <u>merely</u> one of several foods that contain large amounts of carbohydrates.

    (A) only
    (B) slightly
    (C) possibly
    (D) sometimes

23. A new kind of camera <u>incorporates</u> a disc-type film to take fixed-focus photographs.

    (A) rotates
    (B) includes
    (C) monitors
    (D) generates

GO ON TO THE NEXT PAGE ▶

24. The smallest blood vessels in the body are not visible to the <u>naked</u> eye.

    (A) unaided
    (B) trained
    (C) undressed
    (D) damaged

25. The French explorer Sieur de La Salle laid claim to territory in the New World, <u>designating</u> it Louisiana after the French monarch King Louis XIV.

    (A) labeling
    (B) transferring
    (C) acquiring
    (D) unifying

26. A lagoon is formed when coral <u>builds up</u> along a ridge, separating the land from the sea.

    (A) contracts
    (B) disintegrates
    (C) accumulates
    (D) descends

27. Copyright laws are intended to prohibit the systematic <u>reproduction</u> of published works for the purpose of avoiding their purchase.

    (A) revision
    (B) duplication
    (C) preparation
    (D) design

28. Most of the world's languages can be subdivided into <u>vernaculars</u> that are associated with individual ethnic groups.

    (A) conventions
    (B) dialects
    (C) communities
    (D) delineations

29. Jewelry usually contains 14 or 18 karats of gold alloy and rarely is <u>fashioned</u> of pure gold.

    (A) crystallized
    (B) crafted
    (C) adulterated
    (D) refined

30. Stokely Carmichael was leader and spokesperson for the Black Panthers, <u>a militant</u> black-power group of the 1960s.

    (A) a ritualistic
    (B) an ethnic
    (C) a political
    (D) an active

GO ON TO THE NEXT PAGE

Directions: In this part you will read passages on various topics and answer questions about them. Some answers to the questions are directly stated, while others are only suggested.

Read the following passage:

> The pituitary gland, one of the body's key organs, generates a number of hormones that help control body function. Sometimes known as the hypophysis, the gland has two main parts—the anterior lobe and the posterior lobe. It is about the size of a pea and is located near the center of the skull.

Example I

According to the passage, what is another name for the pituitary gland?

(A) The anterior lobe
(B) The hormone
(C) The hypophysis
(D) The posterior lobe

The passage states that the pituitary gland is also known as the hypophysis. Therefore, the correct answer is (C).

Example II

It can be inferred from the passage that the pituitary gland is

(A) quite small
(B) divided into several parts
(C) very large
(D) composed of a number of hormones

The passage states that the pituitary gland is about the size of a pea, which suggests that it is quite small. The correct answer is (A).

Now begin work on the questions.

GO ON TO THE NEXT PAGE

Questions 31–35

Magnetism is an important force of nature acting between objects called magnets. Magnets are most commonly known for their ability to attract metallic substances. The Earth itself behaves as if a large magnet runs through its center, with the strongest areas being at the north and

(5)   south poles. Surprisingly, the magnetic field surrounding the Earth is a million times weaker than the field surrounding an atom, yet it is a million times stronger than that surrounding our own galaxy. Magnetism plays an essential role in creating large amounts of electricity, without which complex industrial techniques would be infeasible.

31. Which of the following is the best title for the passage?

(A) The Uses of Magnets
(B) Important Forces in the Physical World
(C) The Nature of Magnetism
(D) One Source of Electricity

32. According to the passage, magnets are best known

(A) for their role in industry
(B) as a minor process in nature
(C) for the strength of their attraction
(D) for their capacity to draw metallic objects

33. The passage states that the Earth

(A) is immune to magnetic forces
(B) has a large magnet on its surface
(C) acts as if a large magnet runs through its core
(D) has a weak magnetic field at its north and south poles

34. The word "it" in line 6 refers to

(A) an atom's magnetic field
(B) the Earth's surface
(C) the Earth's magnetic field
(D) the galaxy's magnetic field

35. It can be inferred from the passage that

(A) the larger an object, the weaker its magnetic field
(B) the larger an object, the stronger its magnetic field
(C) the smaller an object, the weaker its magnetic field
(D) the strength of a magnetic field is not related to the size of an object

GO ON TO THE NEXT PAGE ➤

111

Questions 36–41

Most educational specialists believe that early schooling should provide children with an awareness of their own abilities and the self-confidence to use these abilities. One approach recognized by many experts as promoting these qualities is the Montessori method, first practiced by Maria

(5) Montessori of Italy in the early 1900s. Nancy McCormick Rambusch is credited with popularizing the method in the United States, where today there are over 400 Montessori schools. The method helps children learn for themselves by providing them with instructional materials and tasks that facilitate acts of discovery and manipulation. Through such exploration,

(10) children develop their sense of touch and learn how to do everyday tasks without adult assistance. Other benefits include improvement in language skills, and acquaintance with elements of science, music, and art.

36. What is the main purpose of this passage?

    (A) To explain the role of early education in child development
    (B) To describe the development of the Montessori method
    (C) To discuss the life and work of Maria Montessori
    (D) To demonstrate how children learn social and cultural values

37. According to the passage, who was first responsible for spreading the Montessori method in the United States?

    (A) Nancy McCormick Rambusch
    (B) A prominent educational expert
    (C) Maria Montessori
    (D) An administrator in the Department of Education

38. In line 9, the word "facilitate" is closest in meaning to which of the following?

    (A) Educate
    (B) Require
    (C) Assist
    (D) Determine

39. Which of the following is NOT mentioned as a benefit of the Montessori method?

    (A) Development of tactile senses
    (B) Improvement of language ability
    (C) Capacity to perform adult tasks
    (D) Knowledge of arts and sciences

GO ON TO THE NEXT PAGE

40. The author of this passage probably feels that the Montessori method

    (A) has little long-lasting benefit for children
    (B) will lose its popularity in the United States
    (C) does not accomplish what it claims to achieve
    (D) is an effective means of child education

41. The following paragraph most likely discusses

    (A) another educational approach beneficial to children
    (B) details on the life of Maria Montessori
    (C) additional practitioners of the Montessori method
    (D) elements of science, music, and art

Questions 42–48

The American Revolutionary War was the result of repeated conflict between the British government and its American colonies. One event that contributed greatly to an escalation in hostilities was the Boston Tea Party of 1773. This incident, in which colonists boarded British ships and
(5)   dumped tea into Boston Harbor, is now a famous milestone in the annals of the American Revolution.

The colonists were reacting to the taxation policies of the British. The Americans had enjoyed a great deal of self-rule until the British government, having completed its takeover of France's empire in North
(10)   America, decided to exercise greater control over colonial activities. When the British instituted the Stamp Tax of 1765 and the Townshend tax on duties in 1767, many colonists simply refused to pay taxes of any kind.

The problem came to a head when the British assigned a monopoly on the import of tea through Boston to individuals sympathetic to their cause.
(15)   The colonists were concerned that this would adversely affect many local merchants and would lead to the creation of monopolies in other retail areas. When the colonial governor, Thomas Hutchinson, refused to prevent tea shipments, about 50 men masquerading as Indians boarded the unguarded British ships, broke apart the chests of tea, and dumped the
(20)   contents into Boston Harbor. The British reacted by sending more troops to support its authority over the colonies, thus increasing the friction even further.

42. The passage is mainly concerned with

(A) the American Revolutionary War
(B) British taxation policies in the colonies
(C) causes of the Boston Tea Party incident
(D) the creation of the American colonies

43. According to the passage, the Boston Tea Party was an important event because

(A) it led to a reduction in taxation by the British
(B) it caused a major increase in conflict with the British
(C) it forced the British to withdraw its troops from the colonies
(D) it prevented the British from importing more tea

44. According to the passage, how did the British first choose to increase control over the colonies?

(A) They limited the amount of self-rule enjoyed by the colonists.
(B) They instituted a series of unpopular tax measures.
(C) They increased their presence in political activities.
(D) They completed their takeover of the French Empire.

GO ON TO THE NEXT PAGE

114

45. In line 13, the expression "came to a head" is used to indicate that

(A) the conflict in the colonies was becoming critical
(B) the problem of monopolies was not serious
(C) some colonists were sympathetic to the British cause
(D) many local businesses were failing

46. The author implies that the colonists dressed as Indians in order to

(A) place the blame on the native Americans
(B) show their alliance with Indian tribes
(C) protect their own identities
(D) frighten the British soldiers on the ships

47. According to the passage, colonists were afraid that the creation of a monopoly in the tea trade would cause

(A) higher prices and even greater taxes on tea
(B) greater British presence in the colonies
(C) the establishment of monopolies in other businesses
(D) adverse effect on domestic tea production

48. It can be inferred from the passage that, prior to the Boston Tea Party incident, British troops

(A) were engaged in constant battles with revolutionaries
(B) had little difficulty in controlling all of North America
(C) were under the command of Governor Thomas Hutchinson
(D) were regularly stationed in colonial America

GO ON TO THE NEXT PAGE

Questions 49–54

The miniscule paramecium is another well-known member of the protozoan family. This one-celled animal, which is hardly detectable without the aid of a microscope, thrives in bodies of fresh water. Like the amoeba, it is composed of a watery substance called protoplasm, which is clear on the
(5)   surface and granular in the interior.
The term "slipper animalcule" is often used to describe the paramecium because its shape resembles that of a shoe. Fine hairs called cilia cover its surface, adding to the appearance of a slipper. The paramecium moves rapidly through water by beating its cilia.
(10)   An interesting feature of the paramecium is its method of reproduction. It divides in two at the middle of its body, and the nucleus in each section divides as well. It then separates into two animals, which may later come together to exchange parts of their nuclei. This process of conjugation demonstrates the beginning stages of sexual reproduction.

49. The previous paragraph most likely discusses

(A) a formerly undiscovered protozoan animal
(B) a member of the protozoan family familiar to many people
(C) members of an animal world containing more than one cell
(D) the characteristics of the amoeba

50. In the second sentence, the phrase "hardly detectable without the aid of a microscope" indicates that a protozoan is

(A) found in all freshwater areas
(B) invisible except in a laboratory setting
(C) so small that it can barely be seen by the eye
(D) unknown to all but the best of scientists

51. According to the passage, what does a paramecium look like?

(A) An amoeba
(B) A fine hair
(C) A shoe
(D) A nucleus

52. It can be inferred from the passage that paramecium are NOT found in

(A) lakes
(B) rivers
(C) ponds
(D) oceans

GO ON TO THE NEXT PAGE

116

53. According to the passage, how does a paramecium move its body?

    (A) By shaking its tail
    (B) By attaching to other moving objects
    (C) By blowing streams of water behind it
    (D) By flailing the fine hairs on its body

54. It can be inferred from the passage that the process of conjugation also applies to

    (A) human reproduction
    (B) the amoeba
    (C) asexual procreation
    (D) nuclear activity

GO ON TO THE NEXT PAGE

Questions 55–60

Alfred Nobel, the famous Swedish chemist who founded the Nobel Prize, was born into a family where research and experimentation were almost second nature. His father Immanuel, out of work and penniless, tested his theories of explosives in a laboratory set up in their house.
(5)   Unfortunately, the elder Nobel remained frustrated in his efforts to apply his natural inventive spirit to establishing a prosperous endeavor.

Alfred Nobel worked alongside his father, and by 1850, when he was 17, Alfred had acquired most of his father's knowledge of and enthusiasm for chemistry. Although numerous other scientists had been intrigued by
(10)   nitroglycerine, Alfred was the one who finally managed to turn this dangerous substance into a safe and useful explosive. He succeeded in developing dynamite commercially, which laid the foundation for many of the world's leading chemical enterprises. Aside from introducing the innovative Nobel Ignitor in 1864 and dynamite in 1866, Alfred claimed 355
(15)   patents including nitrocellulose and substitutes for leather and rubber. He developed clever methods for the production of synthetic silk and was involved in electrochemicals, telecommunications, and safety alarm systems as well.

Alfred Nobel was a dedicated scientist who became very rich applying
(20)   his knowledge of chemistry. His sense of guilt over having created a potentially deadly material led him to leave some of his millions to reward individuals who made substantial contributions to certain areas of science. It was natural that he would include chemistry as one of those branches, especially since the end of the nineteenth century brought rapid
(25)   advancements in the field.

55. Which of the following would be the most appropriate title for the passage?

(A) Alfred Nobel: Inventor of Dynamite
(B) The Chemical Experiments of Alfred Nobel
(C) The Work of Immanuel and Alfred Nobel
(D) Alfred Nobel's Contributions to Chemistry

56. According to the passage, what is true about Alfred Nobel's father Immanuel?

(A) He was never able to capitalize on his work in chemistry.
(B) He was not instrumental in developing his son's enthusiasm for chemistry.
(C) He turned his knowledge of chemistry into a profitable business.
(D) He shared in the work of his son Alfred.

GO ON TO THE NEXT PAGE

57. According to the passage, the power of nitroglycerine

    (A) was first recognized by Immanuel Nobel
    (B) was never utilized well by chemical enterprises
    (C) was most fully developed by Alfred Nobel
    (D) lay in its intrigue for many scientists

58. Which of the following conclusions about Alfred Nobel can be drawn from the passage?

    (A) His talents lay almost exclusively in the area of explosives.
    (B) He was reluctant to bequeath a large part of his wealth towards promoting scientific research.
    (C) He chose to work independently of other scientists.
    (D) He was a major contributor to the rapid progress in chemistry in the late nineteenth century.

59. According to the passage, Alfred Nobel made important progress in developing all of the following items EXCEPT

    (A) nitrocellulose
    (B) rubber and leather
    (C) synthetic silk
    (D) safety alarm devices

60. It can be inferred from the passage that Alfred Nobel later viewed his invention of dynamite

    (A) with much concern for its negative effects on mankind
    (B) as a minor achievement in his long career
    (C) with satisfaction regarding its impact on chemical enterprises
    (D) as a natural outgrowth of his father's training

STOP STOP STOP STOP STOP STOP STOP

Explanations and Answers for Reading Practice Test

Vocabulary

1. (B).
2. (C).
3. (D).
4. (D). *Trans-* is a prefix meaning "across" and *-mit-* is a stem meaning "send." A communicable disease is one that is spread from one person to another.
5. (C).
6. (C). The context provided by the words *adapt* and *urban* points to this answer.
7. (B).
8. (A).
9. (C). *Yet* and *but*, when used as coordinating conjunctions, have the same meaning.
10. (D).
11. (B).
12. (A). *To make up* is an idiom that means "to form, to comprise."
13. (A).
14. (B).
15. (D). The words *mediums* and *means* are synonyms meaning "ways."
16. (A).
17. (C).
18. (A). *Un-* is a negative prefix, which suggests that *erratic*, containing the negative stem *err-*, is the correct choice.
19. (D).
20. (A). The context *in a single direction* suggests this answer.
21. (C).
22. (A).
23. (B). The prefix *-in*, meaning "into," is contained within both the underlined word and the correct answer.
24. (A). *Naked* can mean *undressed*, but not in this context.
25. (A).
26. (C). *To build up* is an idiom.
27. (B).
28. (B). The context *languages* suggests this answer.
29. (B).
30. (D).

Reading Comprehension

Questions 31–35

31. Type: Main Idea
    Key terms: best title
    Answer: (C)

    (C) best describes the overall purpose of the passage. (A). and (D) are too specific, and (B) is too general.

32. Type: Detail
    Key terms: best known
    Answer: (D)

    The answer is in lines 2 and 3.

33. Type: Detail
Key terms: Earth
Answer: (C)

The answer is in lines 3 and 4.

34. Type: Detail
Key terms: it, line 6
Answer: (C)

The answer is in lines 5 and 6.

35. Type: Inference
Key terms: inferred
Answer: (A)

From the information in lines 5–7, you can infer that small objects have strong magnetic fields, while large objects have weak ones.

Questions 36–41

36. Type: Main Idea
Key terms: main purpose
Answer: (B)

(B) accurately identifies the intent of this passage. (A) is mentioned in the first sentence, but only as a general introduction to the passage. (C) and (D) are too specific.

37. Type: Detail
Key terms: who, spreading, method
Answer: (A)

The answer is found in lines 5 and 6.

38. Type: Detail
Key terms: line 9, facilitate, closest in meaning
Answer: (C)

The context in lines 7–9 provides some clue to the meaning.

39. Type: Detail
Key terms: NOT mentioned, benefit
Answer: (C)

The other answers are mentioned in lines 9–12.

40. Type: Inference
Key terms: author, probably feels
Answer: (D)

This answer can be inferred from the positive tone of the passage, especially in lines 3 and 4.

41. Type: Inference
Key terms: following paragraph
Answer: (A)

This answer is suggested by line 3 (''One approach...''). It is a good inference that the next approach will discuss another approach.

42. Type: Main Idea
    Key terms: mainly concerned
    Answer: (C)

    (C) is first mentioned in the second sentence and then developed through the passage. (A) is mentioned in the first sentence as part of the general introduction to the passage. (B) and (D) are not relevant to the topic.

43. Type: Detail
    Key terms: important event
    Answer: (B)

    The answer is in lines 2 and 3.

44. Type: Detail
    Key terms: British, increase control
    Answer: (B)

    The answer can be found in lines 10–12.

45. Type: Detail
    Key terms: line 13, came to a head
    Answer: (A)

    This expression indicates that the problem was becoming very serious. In the context of the passage, (A) is correct.

46. Type: Inference
    Key terms: dressed as Indians
    Answer: (C)

    The answer is suggested by use of the word *masquerading*, which means ''wearing a disguise.''

47. Type: Detail
    Key terms: colonists, afraid, monopoly
    Answer: (C)

    The answer is in lines 15–17.

48. Type: Inference
    Key terms: prior, incident, British troops
    Answer: (D)

    The answer can be inferred from lines 20–22. If the British sent more troops to increase authority, then there must already have been troops in America for this purpose.

Questions 49–54

49. Type: Inference
    Key terms: previous paragraph
    Answer: (B)

    This answer is suggested by line 1 (''another well-known member...'').

122

50. Type: Detail
Key terms: the second sentence, protozoan
Answer: (C)

This answer is a paraphrase of the statement in the second sentence.

51. Type: Detail
Key terms: look like
Answer: (C)

The answer is in line 7. *Resembles* means *looks like*.

52. Type: Inference
Key terms: NOT found
Answer: (D)

Line 3 tells us that the paramecium lives in fresh water. Fresh water is never salty, so it can be inferred that they don't live in oceans.

53. Type: Detail
Key terms: move its body
Answer: (D)

The answer is in line 9. *Flailing* means *beating*, and cilia are the fine hairs on the body of a paramecium.

54. Type: Inference
Key terms: conjugation
Answer: (A)

Lines 13 and 14 suggest that human reproduction is another stage of sexual reproduction.

Questions 55–60

55. Type: Main Idea
Key terms: appropriate title
Answer: (D)

(D) accurately describes the overall purpose of the passage. (A) and (B) are too specific, and (C) is too general.

56. Type: Detail
Key terms: Immanuel
Answer: (A)

The answer is in lines 5 and 6. *To capitalize on one's work* means to turn it into a prosperous endeavor.

57. Type: Detail
Key terms: nitroglycerin
Answer: (C)

The answer is in lines 10–12.

58. Type: Inference
Key terms: conclusions, drawn
Answer: (D)

The second paragraph indicates the contributions that Nobel made during the second half of the nineteenth century. The other answers are not proper conclusions to make.

59. Type: Detail
    Key terms: developing, items, EXCEPT
    Answer: (B)

    The other answers are mentioned in lines 15–17. Nobel worked on substitutes for rubber and leather, not on rubber and leather themselves.

60. Type: Inference
    Key terms: viewed, dynamite
    Answer: (A)

    This answer is suggested in lines 20–22.

TEST OF WRITTEN ENGLISH

The Test of Written English (TWE) is a separate section of the TOEFL administered in March, May, September, and October. It is used to determine your ability to write clearly in English. You have 30 minutes to prepare and write a 200- to 300-word essay on a topic that is given to you.

The TWE is different from Section 2, Part B (Written Expression) in that the TWE requires direct production of written English. Section 2 tests only indirect recognition of errors in written English.

Your score on the TWE is separate from your score on the three main sections of the TOEFL. At the present time, the TWE result does not affect your overall TOEFL score in any way. Your TWE score can range from 1 (poor) to 6 (excellent).

Types of Questions

- There are two types of essay questions that are often used in an academic setting. These questions generally require you to:

  a. compare/contrast opposite viewpoints and argue for one viewpoint or the other; OR
  b. analyze and explain a chart or graph.

  The TWE uses two kinds of questions because they are typical of the ones you will have to answer in college courses.

- Here is an example of an essay question that requires you to COMPARE/CONTRAST:

MODEL 1

Some people believe that individuals should not be allowed to own handguns. Other people believe that gun ownership is an important personal right. Write a brief essay in which you discuss each of these positions. Give two or three advantages and disadvantages of gun ownership and explain which position you support.

- Here is an example of an essay question that requires you to ANALYZE AND EXPLAIN A CHART.

<u>MODEL 2</u>

Americans 65 and over
Total population in millions, showing percentage of elderly, 1900-2020

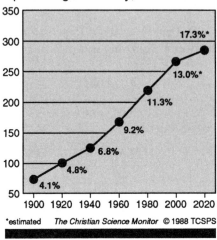

*estimated   *The Christian Science Monitor* © 1988 TCSPS

Source: US Census Bureau

Instructions: Suppose you are to write a report in which you interpret this graph. Discuss how the information on total population is related to the percentage of elderly people. Explain the conclusions you have reached from the information in the graph. Be certain that the graph supports your points.

General Considerations

- For an essay that requires you to compare/contrast, you should:

  a. support your ideas with examples for each viewpoint;
  b. explain your own opinion on an issue.

- For an essay that requires you to interpret a chart/graph, you should:

  a. support your ideas with facts from the chart or graph;
  b. make valid conclusions from the facts.

- For both kinds of essay questions, it is important for you to:

  a. organize your ideas carefully before writing;
  b. answer the question thoroughly in your essay;
  c. write clearly in academic English.

- The best way to write clearly is to use grammatical structures and vocabulary that you know well. You should write simply and correctly with as few errors as possible.

- You should try to use correct grammar, punctuation, and vocabulary, but these are not as important as the organization and presentation of your essay.

Preparing Your Essay

Before writing your essay, you should spend a few minutes organizing your ideas. The TWE includes space for you to write some brief notes on the topic.

- The best way to organize your thoughts is to write an outline. The typical outline is one that shows your main ideas and supporting details in the order you will present them.

- The following is a standard outline on the issue of handgun ownership (Model 1):

    I. Introduction—issue of handgun ownership
        A. Some people believe individuals should not own handguns
        B. Others believe ownership is an important personal right

    II. Disadvantages of handgun ownership
        A. Adults and children can have accidents
        B. People can use for crimes

    III. Advantages of handgun ownership
        A. People can protect themselves from intruders
        B. People can use for recreational purposes

    IV. Personal Opinion
        A. Problems of accidents and crime make gun ownership difficult to accept
        B. Gun ownership should not be allowed in the interest of a better society

- This standard outline uses Roman numerals (I, II, etc.), capital letters (A, B, etc.), and complete sentences. However, since you don't have much time on the TWE, it is better to use an abbreviated outline such as the following:

    Introduction
        Some people believe no indiv. handgun ownership
        Others believe owning imp. right

    Disadvantages
        Contribute to accidents
        Used for crime

    Advantages
        Self-protection
        Recreation

    Personal Opinion
        Serious problems of crime and accidents
        Should not be allowed

- The following is an abbreviated outline for an essay interpreting the chart on elderly Americans (Model 2).

    Introduction
        Population of U.S. increasing steadily
        Elderly are a growing percentage
        Pattern estimated to change in future

    1960–1980
        Pop. from 170 mill. to 210 mill.
        % of elderly from 9.2% to 11.3%
        Same as for previous years

1980–2000
    Pop. from 210 mill. to 260 mill., slightly faster
    % of elderly from 11.3% to 13%, greater increase

2000–2020
    Pop. from 260 mill. to 280 mill., much slower
    % of elderly from 13% to 17.3%, much faster

Conclusion
    More difficult for young to support elderly
    Gov't. social programs needed

Writing Your Essay

- When you write your essay, follow your outline carefully. A well-organized outline helps to create a well-written essay.

- The first paragraph of your essay introduces the general topic. It also gives some idea of the examples or facts that will be used. The first paragraph should contain three to four sentences that clearly show what the essay will discuss.

- The body of your essay consists of two to three paragraphs that develop the general topic. Each paragraph should have its own specific topic. All the sentences in a paragraph must be related to the specific topic.

- The last paragraph should include either your own opinion on an issue (for an essay that compares/contrasts) or some valid conclusions (for an essay interpreting a chart).

- Read the following essays based on the two Models and study the analyses after each essay.

Model Essay 1

    People cannot agree on the issue of handgun ownership. Some believe that individuals should not be allowed to own handguns. Others believe that gun ownership is an important personal right. Each side has good arguments for its point of view.
    People who are against handgun ownership are concerned about the problems guns cause. They point to the accidents that happen when adults use their guns or when children play with them without parental knowledge. They also believe that the rate of crime is directly related to the number of privately-owned handguns. They are especially upset about crimes of passion, which could involve the death or injury of a family member after a big argument.
    People who support handgun ownership are interested in maintaining this personal privilege. They believe that citizens should be able to protect their homes and families from outside intruders. They also enjoy using guns for hunting, target practice, and other recreational purposes. They are strong believers in the traditional rights of the individual.
    Guns have been a necessary part of life for most of history, but today's society is quite different. The serious problems of crime and family conflicts have made gun ownership difficult to accept. Private ownership of handguns should not be allowed in the interest of creating a better society for all people.

Analysis

The first paragraph introduces the general topic of handgun ownership. It mentions the disagreement on this issue, and indicates that the arguments will be discussed.

The second paragraph discusses the disadvantages of handgun ownership. It mentions the problem of accidents among adults and children. It also associates gun ownership with crime, especially crimes of passion involving families.

The third paragraph discusses the advantages of handgun ownership. It mentions the importance of protecting family and home from intruders. It indicates the use of guns for recreational purposes. It states the traditional right of individuals to own guns.

The fourth paragraph concludes that society today is different from the past. Serious social problems make gun ownership unacceptable. The conclusion states clearly that gun ownership should not be allowed.

Model Essay 2

The population of the United States has been increasing at a steady rate since the early 1900s. At the same time, the percentage of the elderly in the population has grown as well. However, future estimates point to a major pattern change during the next 30 years.

From 1960 to 1980, the population of the United States grew from 170 million to 210 million. For the same period, the percentage of the elderly in the population rose from 9.2 percent to 11.3 percent. Both increases were about the same as for previous 20-year intervals.

From 1980 to 2000, the U.S. population is expected to jump from 210 million to 260 million. The percentage of elderly people is estimated to climb from 11.3 percent to 13 percent. Compared to previous intervals, population will increase more quickly while the percentage of the elderly increases more slowly.

From 2000 to 2020, the U.S. population is estimated to rise by only 20 million, from 260 million to 280 million. However, the percentage of the elderly will jump dramatically, from 13 percent to 17.3 percent. These figures indicate a major change from the pattern of previous years.

If these estimates prove correct, the elderly will form a much larger portion of the U.S. population. This means that it will probably be difficult for young working people to support elderly people properly. It may be necessary for the U.S. government to provide additional social programs and services for the elderly to have comfortable lives.

Analysis

The first paragraph introduces the general topic of population growth and mentions the important change in pattern estimated for the next 30 years.

The second, third, and fourth paragraphs analyze the facts for three different 20-year intervals. The fourth paragraph discusses the major change expected in the future.

The fifth paragraph draws conclusions based on the information in the chart. One conclusion is that working people will have problems supporting the elderly. The other conclusion is that the U.S. government will have to do more for the elderly.

General Analysis of Both Model Essays

- An essay that requires you to compare/contrast will usually consist of four paragraphs. The paragraphs could be summarized as follows:

Introduction
Advantages of X
Disadvantages of X
Personal Opinion

- An essay requiring you to interpret a graph could consist of four or five paragraphs. The choice will depend on the type of graph and the information in it. For Model Essay 2, a five-paragraph format was used:

Introduction
Period from 1960 to 1980
Period from 1980 to 2000
Period from 2000 to 2020
Conclusions

Many charts and graphs show change over time, so the paragraphs in the body of your essay could be organized around these time periods.

Strategies for the TWE

- You have 30 minutes to write a 200-word to 300-word essay. You should spend 5–10 minutes preparing an outline and 20–25 minutes writing the essay.

- Remember to stick to the topic. This means that every sentence must be related to the subject. Do not include ideas that do not support your point.

- Do not try to write very complicated sentences or to use difficult vocabulary. Use grammatical structures and words that you are already familiar with. The organization of your essay is more important than the forms in it.

Writing Practice

You can use the following sample topics to practice writing essays. You should try to find a native speaker of English who has taught writing classes, and ask this person to give you advice on the organization of your essays.

1. Some people enjoy living in foreign countries. Others would never consider living abroad. Discuss the advantages and disadvantages of living abroad and give your own opinion.
2. Some people believe that raising children is an important part of life. Others prefer not to raise any children. Discuss the advantages and disadvantages of raising children and give your own opinion.
3. Some young adults continue to live with their parents while attending college. Others insist on having their own apartment. Discuss the benefits of living at home and the benefits of having one's own place. Be sure to state your personal opinion.
4. The chart on the next page shows the various sources of radiation in the world. Discuss the information in the chart as it relates to the dangers of radiation for humans. Be sure to support your conclusions with details from the chart.

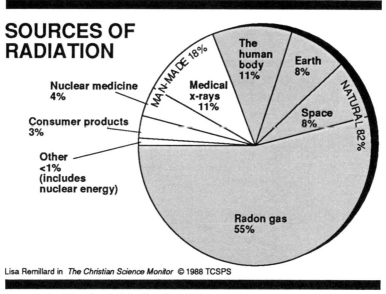

SOURCES OF RADIATION

Nuclear medicine 4%

Consumer products 3%

Other <1% (includes nuclear energy)

MAN-MADE 18%

Medical x-rays 11%

The human body 11%

Earth 8%

Space 8%

NATURAL 82%

Radon gas 55%

Lisa Remillard in *The Christian Science Monitor* © 1988 TCSPS

Source: National Council on Radiation Protection and Measurements

5. The following chart shows the support that various American presidents received from the U.S. Congress. In your essay, summarize the information in the chart and justify your conclusions.

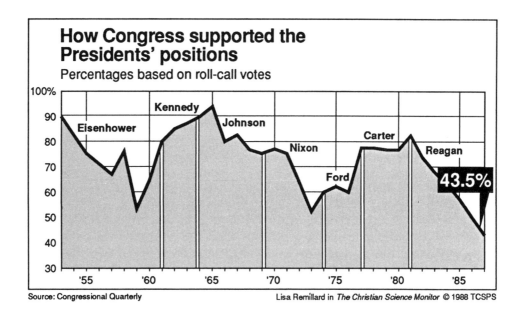

How Congress supported the Presidents' positions

Percentages based on roll-call votes

Eisenhower Kennedy Johnson Nixon Ford Carter Reagan 43.5%

Source: Congressional Quarterly

Lisa Remillard in *The Christian Science Monitor* © 1988 TCSPS

6. The following chart shows the amount of money spent on advertising in two major mediums, television and newspapers. Discuss the pattern shown in the chart and support your conclusions with facts.

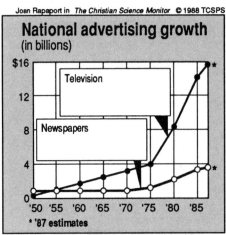

Joan Rapaport in *The Christian Science Monitor* © 1988 TCSPS

National advertising growth
(in billions)

Television

Newspapers

'87 estimates

Sources: McCann Erickson, Newspaper Advertising Bureau, Television Bureau of Advertising

APPENDIX A

LISTENING APPENDIX

Ways to Improve Your Listening Ability

By following the suggestions below, you can improve your listening ability greatly. Your success is limited only by the number of opportunities you have and the effort you make.

1. Make an effort to have conversations with English speakers.

- There is no substitute for real interaction with native English speakers. Speaking your own language with friends will do nothing to help you learn English.

- If you live in an English-speaking country, you can make friends with people you meet near your residence or on campus. If it is difficult (or almost impossible) for you to do this, then try to have brief discussions with people you meet at the store, bank, supermarket, beach—anywhere you can.

- English speakers live and work in almost every country in the world. Although you may have more difficulty finding such people, take advantage of every chance you have to meet and talk.

2. Watch television and listen to the radio as much as possible.

- Television (TV) and radio are excellent means of improving your listening skills. TV is the most useful because the picture helps you to understand the language.

- English-speaking countries offer the most opportunities for you. However, many other countries have English-language TV and radio broadcasts as well.

- The best shows on television to watch are: nightly newscasts and special news reports, talk shows, soap operas (ongoing dramas), game shows, and situation comedies. Newscasts and reports are particularly good for listening to standard, formal English; situation comedies are very good for learning slang and idiomatic expressions.

3. Use the telephone as a tool for obtaining information.

- In English-speaking countries, there are many places that have recorded messages (such as movie theaters, stores that are closed, the weather bureau), which provide easy opportunities to listen without having to speak.

- You can also call some business that is open and ask real questions, such as ''What are your hours on weekdays?'' or ''Do you have any TOEFL books available?'' A bookstore would be the appropriate place to call about TOEFL books, but it might be interesting to call a department store instead, just to hear what the answer is!

Common Idiomatic Expressions

Some idioms must have an object following the verb. These cases are indicated by (someone) or (something). Alternate idiomatic forms are indicated by brackets after the definition.

to ask (someone) out   to invite on a date   **[to take out]**
If you like her, you should ask her out on a date.

to ask (someone) over   to invite to one's home   **[to have over]**
My wife and I asked the new neighbors over for dinner.

to back out of   to withdraw from
The company president changed his mind and backed out of the project.

to be about   to have as a purpose   **[to have to do with]**
Could you tell me what this book is about?

to be about to   to just begin to   **[to be going to]**
She was about to take a shower when the telephone rang.

to be against   to oppose, not to agree with
I'd be glad to explain why I'm against your plan.

to be back   to return   **[to come back, to get back]**
You're going to be back soon, aren't you?
Yeah, I'll get back in an hour or so.

to be behind   to be late, to delay   **[to run behind]**
I hate to be behind in my studies, but I usually am anyway.

to be beyond   not to be understood by
That professor's lecture was beyond me!

to be booked up   to have no rooms remaining
I'm sorry, sir, but the hotel is all booked up.

to be bound to   to be likely or probable to
If you work hard, you're bound to succeed.

to be for (something)   to support, to agree with   **[to go for]**
I'm sorry to tell you that I'm for his idea.

to be from   to originate from (a country)   **[to come from]**
Oh, so you're from Canada; I come from France.

to be in   to be at work or at home
I'd like to make an appointment; when is Mr. Smith going to be in?

to be in on   to participate in, to be involved in
Martha's a sociable person, so she's in on most school activities.

to be off   not to function
The lights should be off when no one's in the room.

to be on   (a) to function
Why are the lights on? The sun is shining!

                                 (b) to be planned or scheduled
I think that the meeting is still on for tomorrow.

                                 (c) to be paid for by
Don't get out your money; this meal is on me.

to be out   to be gone from work or home   [to be away]
Yesterday I went to visit him, but he was out.

to be out of   not to have, to lack   [to run out of]
Joe needed an umbrella, but the store was out of them.

to be over   to be finished   [to get over]
I hope that this movie is over soon; it's so boring!

to be up   (a) to be awake   [to stay up]
Boy, I'm tired. I was up all night studying.

                                 (b) to be happening (in greeting)   [to go on]
                                 (often used with *what* in a question)
Hi, Karen. What's up?

to be up to   (a) to be the decision of   [to leave it up to]
I don't care where we go. Really, it's up to you.

                                 (b) to be doing
I haven't seen Terry in a long time; I wonder what she's up to.

                                 (c) to be able to do   [to feel up to]
You look sick, John. Are you up to going to the party?

to break down   to fail to work properly   [to fall apart]
You should get a new car before your old one breaks down.

to break in   to interrupt unexpectedly   [to cut in]
The secretary broke in to tell her boss of an important call.

to break up   to stop (a relationship or activity)
Do you know why Cynthia and Bob broke up?
The meeting broke up after hours of argument but no decisions.

to bring on   to cause
Too much hard work can bring on a headache.

to bring up   (a) to raise (children)
The child was brought up in a good home environment.

(b) to mention or introduce
The student brought up an interesting point in class.

to brush up on   to practice or review
You'd better brush up on your French before going to Paris.

to build up   to increase, to accumulate
The amount of pollution in the atmosphere is building up rapidly.

to burn out   to tire completely, to exhaust
All this work has burned me out; let's take a nap.

to burn (someone) up   to anger, to upset
It really burns me up that he never does what he says he will.

to call (someone) back   to respond to a phone call   **[to get back to]**
I told her you'd call her back soon.

to call off   to cancel
Class was called off because the professor was sick.

to call on   to visit
When is the best time to call on them?

to call up   to call on the telephone
I called up an old friend when I visited his hometown.

to care for   to like, to enjoy
Would you care for a cup of tea?

to catch on to   to understand
Either I couldn't catch on to his joke or it really wasn't funny.

to catch up on   to work to meet a requirement   **[to make up]**
Because she took a two-week vacation, she had to catch up on her work.

to catch up with   to become equal to others
That guy is the fastest runner in the race; I'll never catch up with him.

to check in   to register (at a hotel)
Guests are alllowed to check in at 3 P.M.

to check out   (a) to inform a hotel when leaving
The businessman inquired about the checkout time.

          (b) to investigate, to inspect
The customers checked out the new car carefully before buying it.

to clear up   (a) to become sunny
Oh, look—the weather's cleared up. Now we can go on that picnic.

(b) to make understandable, to remove doubt

The clerk tried to clear up the problem with the customer.

to come about   to happen   **[to take place]**

The policeman inquired about how the accident came about.

to come down with   to get an illness

I feel like I'm coming down with a cold.

to come to a head   to become serious, to reach a critical point

The political situation came to a head when the president resigned.

to come up with   to think of, to discover

I've come up with an idea; let's ask my Mom for her advice.

to count (someone) in   to include (as a participant)

Berry told us to count him in on the project.

to count out   not to include, to exclude

Sally won't have anything to do with our plan, so count her out.

to cut it out   to stop (usually a command)   **[to knock it off]**

Hey, Larry, cut it out. I'm not amused.

to do (something) over   to repeat, to do again

The teacher asked several students to do their assignments over.

to do without   to live without something

How are you going to do without any money for two weeks?

to dress up   to put good clothes on

We'd better dress up for the party. My supervisor will be there.

to drive at   to suggest indirectly, to hint   **[to get at]**

What are you driving at? Please be more clear.

to drop by   to visit unexpectedly   **[to drop in on]**

Oh, it was nice of you to drop by like this.

to drop out of   to stop attending

Did you hear that Mac dropped out of school last week?

to eat out   to eat at a restaurant

I don't feel like cooking tonight. Let's eat out, OK?

to fall through   to fail, not to occur (as a plan)

The businessman flew home when the real estate deal fell through.

to be fed up with   to be unable to accept anymore

Vera was fed up with arguing with her roommates.

to feel like   to desire to
Do you feel like staying home or going out for a while?

to figure out   to solve, to find (an answer)   **[to work out]**
It took him a long time to figure out the answer to the question.

to fill in   (a) to substitute (for a person)
Professor Jones asked her assistant to fill in for her that day.

                                   (b) to tell, to inform
The secretary filled in her boss on what had happened while he was away.

                                   (c) to write an answer (on an empty line)
Please think carefully as you fill in the blanks.

to fill out   to complete (a form or application)
Use a pen to fill out this employment application.

to fill up   (a) to fill completely
Could you fill up the gas tank and check the oil, too?

                                   (b) to satisfy one's hunger
Boy, that meal really filled me up.

to find out   to learn, to discover
The detective reported what he had found out about the criminal.

to fit the bill   to be suitable, to match
I love this new sofa in our living room; it really fits the bill.

to fly   to pass quickly (for time)   **[to go by]**
Time sure flies when you're having fun.

to fool around   (a) to waste time   **[to screw around]**
Isn't it time you stopped fooling around and started working?

                                   (b) to joke
Don't take me seriously; I'm just fooling around.

to get along with   to live or associate well with
How are you getting along with your new roommates?

to get in   (a) to arrive
The plane got in an hour ahead of schedule.

                                   (b) to enter (a car, a truck)
Six people were able to get in the compact car.

to get off   to leave (a bus, a plane, a train)
Mary was anxious to get off the plane and see her husband.

to get (a problem) off   to talk openly about
one's chest
John got the problem off his chest when he talked to his parents.

to get on   to enter (a bus, a plane, a train)
Oh, look, it's time to get on the bus. Let's hurry.

to get on (it)   to start work on (something) immediately
When the police received word of the crime, they got on it right away.

to get out of   to leave (a car, a truck)
The policemen politely asked them to get out of the car.

to get over   to recover from (an illness)
I hope you get over your cold in time to attend the reception.

to get rid of   to discard   **[to throw out, to throw away]**
Mrs. Jones got rid of all her old clothes during the garage sale.

to get up   to arise from bed, to awake from sleep
What time do you usually get up in the morning?

to get used to   to adapt to, to become accustomed to
She still hasn't gotten used to the noise of the big city.

to give away   to distribute at no charge
You mean it costs a dollar? I thought they were giving it away!

to give off   to release, to emit
Chemical factories often give off a bad smell in the air.

to give the time of day   to pay attention to (usually negative)
I was surprised that the new director didn't give us the time of day.

to give up   to stop (a bad habit)
His bad heart and liver forced him to give up drinking.

to go ahead   to continue, to resume   **[to go on]**
I didn't mean to interrupt; please go ahead.

to go along with   (a) to agree with, to accept
The few people who disagreed had to go along with the majority vote.

        (b) to accompany (on an activity)
That sounds like fun; can I go along with you?

to go by   to visit briefly   **[to stop by]**
Martha went by the store to get some milk and eggs.

to go in for   to enjoy (as a hobby or sport)
Vance didn't know that Bill went in for soccer, too.

to go on to happen (used with *what*)
What's going on? Why are you making so much noise?

to go through (a) to eat or use all of something [to use up]
Mrs. James was amazed that the children had gone through the cookies.

(b) to endure, to suffer
The heart patient went through several difficult operations.

to go up to increase (in price)
Automobile prices are expected to go up 10 percent this year.

to go with to look good with, to match [to go together]
Do you think that this blouse goes with this skirt?

to grow up to mature (from child to adult)
Children grow up as they acquire more experience and knowledge.

to hand in to submit, to return
At the end of the exam period, the students handed in their tests.

to hand out to distribute [to pass out]
The teacher talked informally as she handed out the material.

to hang around to stay at one's usual place
During vacation Sue decided to hang around home and relax.

to hang on to wait, to be patient [to hold on]
Hang on a minute! Don't be so impatient.
The operator told me to hang on while she placed the call.

to hang up to stop talking on the telephone
It was obvious that Carl was angry from the way he hung up the phone.

to have on to be wearing
The first day he came to work, he had on a business suit.

to hear from to receive a letter or phone call from
Have you heard from your parents in Europe yet?

to hold it against (someone) to resent someone for doing something in the past
Jan didn't mean to wreck your car; you shouldn't hold it against her.

to hold up to delay
Sorry I'm late. The traffic held me up.

to keep after to remind constantly
The little boy's mother had to keep after him to wash his hands.

to lay aside to save or store for the future [to set aside]
Every month he lay aside $100 to buy a new car.

to lay off   to release from a job   **[to let go]**
The employer regretted having to lay off several of her employees.

to lay up   to restrict to one place
The bad illness laid him up in bed for several days.

to lean on   to rely on, to depend on
He leaned on his friends for advice after his wife died.

to leave behind   not to take (when leaving)
The student left his books behind in the classroom.

to leave out   to omit, not to include
I want to hear your whole story; don't leave out any details.

to leave (it) to   to make (someone) responsible for
You shouldn't do that work; leave it to Bill to do.

to let (someone) down   to disappoint
Mary really let Tom down when she failed to attend the reception.

to let go of   to release, to loosen one's grasp
Don't let go of the railing as you go down those steep stairs.

to live up to   to meet someone's expected standards
Sam lived up to his parent's expectations by doing well in school.

to look after   to watch, to protect   **[to take care of]**
Could you look after my bike while I run into the store?

to look back on   to recall something from the past
When I look back on my childhood, I have fond memories.

to look into   to investigate
The bank looked into the matter of the missing million dollars.

to look up to   to respect, to admire
A professor is someone you should be able to look up to.

to make out   to understand, to see or read clearly
It was so noisy that they couldn't make out what the man said.
Can you make out the letters on that sign over there?

to make up   (a) to create (something untrue)
The Thompsons made up an excuse for not attending the party.

                            (b) to comprise, to be composed of
Fifty states make up the United States of America.

                            (c) to fulfill an obligation later
Several students missed the exam and had to make it up.

(d) to apply cosmetics

Women make up their faces to enhance their appearance; they use many different kinds of makeup.

to mean to   to intend to

The child said that he didn't mean to break the window.

to mix up   to confuse or bewilder

What street is this? I'm all mixed up.

to open up   to speak honestly, to show one's feelings

It's hard to understand Sean because he doesn't open up to anyone.

to pay back   to return borrowed money

Hey, you still owe me $20; when can you pay me back?

to pick on   (a) to choose someone to respond

The teacher picked on several students to answer her questions.

(b) to mistreat, to tease

The older boys picked on the younger ones.

to pick out   to select, to choose

The shopper picked out the best strawberries for himself.

to pick up   to get or buy something

We should stop by the store and pick up some eggs and milk.

to point out   to indicate, to show

I'd like to point out the advantages of investing in the stock market.

to pull (someone's) leg   to tease, to annoy   [to put (someone) on]

She was pulling my leg when she said she won a million dollars.

to put away   to clean, to remove from sight

Johnny! Put those clothes away right now!

to put back   to return to a proper place

Please put those books back when you're done.

to put off   to postpone

It's getting late; let's put off this matter until tomorrow.

to put on   to place on the body

It's cold outside. You'd better put on a jacket.

to put (someone) through   to support financially

Carla's parents put her through college for four years.

to put up with   to accept an unpleasant situation

It's too bad Jackie has to put up with a disagreeable neighbor.

to rip off   to rob, to steal from
A thief has ripped off several banks in the college area.

to see off   to go with someone to the airport, bus station, etc.
It was fun to see Betty and Karl off yesterday.

to settle down   (a) to live a normal, routine life
After years of partying, he has finally settled down with someone.

           (b) to become quiet and calm
Children, you're making too much noise! Settle down or else!

to set up   to establish; to found
The employee left the company and set up his own business.

to show off   to act in a way to get others' attention
Look at John lifting that big rock. He's showing off again.

to show up   to appear, to attend
It is best to show up to a business meeting on time.

to sign up   to register
At the start of the semester, students have to sign up for classes.

to sleep on it   to consider something important for a while
Jack couldn't decide which job to take. He had to sleep on it for several days.

to speak up   (a) to talk more loudly or clearly
I couldn't hear you. Speak up!

           (b) to express one's opinions
In class discussions, a teacher wants students to speak up.

to stay up   to remain awake, not to sleep
During finals week, students stay up late to study.

to take after   to resemble or look like another person
Fred takes after his father in physical features, but he takes after his mother in personality.

to take it easy   to relax, not to be upset (usually a command)
Why are you so upset? Take it easy!

to take off   (a) to remove (clothing)
It's too warm in here. Take off your sweater.

           (b) to leave someplace
Well, it's getting late. I'd better take off.

to take place   to happen, to occur
When will the next meeting with the Board of Directors take place?

to talk (someone) into   to persuade or convince to do something
Mac didn't want to do it, but his friends talked him into it.

to talk over   to discuss (some problem)
They talked over the matter several times, but could never agree.

to think of   to have as an opinion
What do you think of the policies of the present government?

to think (something) over   to consider carefully
Before I decide, I want to think it over; I'll let you know soon.

to tie (someone) down   to limit or restrict one's activities
Jeff likes to travel, but his family and job really tie him down.

to touch on   to discuss briefly
Before the exam, the teacher touched on the important points.

to turn down   (a) to decrease the loudness of
I'm talking on the phone; please turn down the radio.

        (b) to refuse an offer
The young woman turned down the invitation from a stranger.

to turn off   to make something stop working
Please turn off the lights before you leave the room.

to turn on   to make something work
To turn on the computer, move this switch to the right.

to turn up   to increase the volume of
The sound of the tape recorder was unclear, so they turned it up.

to wait on   to serve (in a restaurant)
We had to sit for ten minutes before someone waited on us.

to wait up for   to remain awake until someone returns.
The teenager's parents were so worried that they waited up for her.

to wear off   to disappear slowly
It took several weeks for the effects of my illness to wear off.

to wear out   (a) to use something until it is useless
The needle on Jack's record player wore out, so he replaced it.

        (b) to exhaust
The soccer players were worn out from the practice session.

to work out   (a) to reach an agreement, to solve a problem
The Johnsons were able to save their marriage by working their problems out.

        (b) to exercise
To keep in shape, you should work out at least twice a week.

APPENDIX B

STRUCTURE APPENDIX

Clauses and Phrases

A. Main Clauses

1. A MAIN CLAUSE is a set of words that:

   a. has a main subject and a main verb; and
   b. is a correct sentence by itself.

   <u>The Gothic Movement</u>   <u>occurred</u>   during the 1800s.
   MAIN SUBJECT   MAIN VERB

2. A main clause may include other parts of grammar (such as the phrase *during the 1800s* in the example above). Also, the main subject and verb may be separated.

   <u>Alcohol,</u>   a depressant drug,   <u>lowers</u>   activity.
   MAIN SUBJECT   MAIN VERB

3. Two or more main clauses can be joined together by using the COORDINATING CONJUNCTIONS *and, but, or, so, yet*, and *for*. These words are CLAUSE MARKERS (CMs) because they introduce a clause.

   <u>Some metals are pliable,</u>   <u>but</u>   <u>others are fragile.</u>
   MAIN CLAUSE   CM   MAIN CLAUSE

   A coordinating conjunction can occur only in middle position.

4. A special problem with the main verb is whether it should be ACTIVE or PASSIVE. Here is a main clause with an ACTIVE verb:

   <u>(Henry) Ford</u>   <u>revolutionized</u>   <u>the automobile industry.</u>
   SUBJECT   ACTIVE VERB   OBJECT

   Notice that an active verb is followed by an OBJECT. Both of these are necessary to make a passive sentence. The steps to making a passive sentence are:

   a. Switch the subject and object; add *by* in front of the subject.

   1st step: <u>The automobile industry</u> revolutionized <u>by Ford</u> .

   b. Change the active verb to a past participle (*-ed*) form; often this looks the same as the past tense. Also, add the verb *to be* in the same tense that the active verb had.

   2nd step: The automobile industry <u>was revolutionized</u> by Ford.

   c. Sometimes the *by* phrase is not needed:

   Wildlife preserves <u>are intended</u> (by people) to protect endangered species.

5. Another special problem with main verbs occurs when the main clause begins with a negative word. In such cases, the sentence after the negative word must be in QUESTION FORM. This is necessary with the following forms:

   a. NOT ONLY... but also

   <u>Not only</u> have nuclear weapons resulted in vast expense, but also they have endangered human existence.

b. NOT ONLY... as well

Not only have nuclear weapons resulted in vast expense, but they have endangered human existence as well.

This is an alternate form of (a).

c. NOT UNTIL

Not until the early 1900s did medical advances reduce infant mortality substantially.

d. RARELY

Rarely can a politician fulfill all campaign promises.

e. ONLY SOMETIMES

Only sometimes do tropical storms reach northern areas.

f. NEVER

Never will scientists find a means of ensuring immortality.

g. SELDOM

Seldom do art critics consider movies to be a form of fine art.

B. Subordinate Clauses

1. A SUBORDINATE CLAUSE is a set of words that:

   a. has its own clause subject and clause verb;
   b. is introduced by a clause marker (CM); and
   c. is not a correct sentence by itself.

Although birds are warm blooded,   they are not mammals.

CM

SUBORDINATE CLAUSE   MAIN CLAUSE

2. A subordinate clause must occur with a main clause. Clause markers are used to connect subordinate clauses to main clauses. The most common clause markers are listed below.

C. Common Clause Markers

Set 1   after, although, as, as soon as, because, before, even though, if, since, though, unless, until, when, whether, while

1. These clause markers (CMs) are SUBORDINATING CONJUNCTIONS. They are used to introduce one kind of subordinate clause. This kind of subordinate clause can occur before or after the main clause.

John F. Kennedy was still a young man   when he was killed.

CM

MAIN CLAUSE   SUBORDINATE CLAUSE

When he was killed,   John F. Kennedy was still a young man.

CM

SUBORDINATE CLAUSE   MAIN CLAUSE

2. The choice of form depends on the desired relationship (contrast, reason/result, time, etc.) between the main clause and subordinate clause.

   a. TIME

   John F. Kennedy was killed when he was still a young man.

b. CONTRAST

Although some metals are pliable, others are very fragile.

c. REASON

Richard Nixon resigned the U.S. presidency because he was disgraced by the Watergate scandal.

Set 2 who, whom, whose, which, that

1. These clause markers (CMs) are called RELATIVE PRONOUNS. They introduce a relative clause, which modifies a noun in some way. A relative clause is another kind of subordinate clause.

<pre>
The person   who regulates state finances   is a comptroller.
  NOUN   CM
                RELATIVE CLAUSE
</pre>

2. A relative clause acts like an adjective because it describes a noun such as *person*. A relative clause is also called an ADJECTIVE CLAUSE.

3. *Who, whom*, and *whose* are used for PEOPLE;

Which is for ANIMALS/THINGS;

That is used for PEOPLE/ANIMALS/THINGS.

4. *Who, whom, which*, and *that* occur as subjects or objects of relative clauses; *whose* is a possessive adjective.

a. Example of *who*:

<pre>
The person   who   regulates state finances   is a comptroller.
 MAIN   SUBJECT
 SUBJECT   RELATIVE CLAUSE
</pre>

This sentence is formed from two sentences:

a. The person is a comptroller.
b. The person regulates state finances.

Who can be replaced by *that*:

The person that regulates state finances is a comptroller.

b. Example of *whom*:

<pre>
Court justices   whom   a governor appoints   serve for life.
MAIN SUBJECT   OBJECT
                     RELATIVE CLAUSE
</pre>

This sentence is formed from two sentences:

a. Court justices serve for life.
b. A governor appoints court justices.

Whom can be replaced by *that*.

Court justices that a governor appoints serve for life.

c. Example of *whose*:

A bird   whose   nest is disturbed   will abandon it.
MAIN   ADJ.
SUBJECT   CM
_____
RELATIVE CLAUSE

This sentence comes from two sentences:

a. A bird will abandon it (the bird's nest).
b. The bird's nest is disturbed.

Whose CANNOT be replaced by *that* because it is not a subject or object of the clause; it is an adjective.

d. Examples of *which*:

Jet streams are layers of air   which   move rapidly above earth.
                 SUBJECT
                    RELATIVE CLAUSE

Laws   which   Congress passes   can be vetoed by the president.
     OBJECT
       RELATIVE CLAUSE

Sentences with *which* are formed from two sentences in the same way as those with *who*. *Which* can also be replaced by *that*.

Jet streams are layers of air <u>that</u> move rapidly above earth.
Laws <u>that</u> Congress passes can be vetoed by the president.

5. As you can see, *that* is a very useful form. For this reason, it commonly occurs on the TOEFL test.

Set 3 how, how many, how much, what, when, where, why; who, whom, whose, which

1. These clause markers are called INFORMATION WORDS. They introduce a noun clause that is the subject or object of a sentence. A noun clause is another kind of subordinate clause.

How much   the Russian government spends on defense   is secret.
   CM
_____
     NOUN CLAUSE/SUBJECT

No one can predict   when   an earthquake will strike.
               CM
               NOUN CLAUSE/OBJECT

2. Notice that relative pronouns become INFORMATION words when they introduce a noun clause, not an adjective clause.

Historians now know   who   Jack the Ripper probably was.
                 CM
                 NOUN CLAUSE/OBJECT

In this case, *that* cannot replace *who*.

Set 4 that (complement form)

1. This clause marker is a COMPLEMENTIZER. It introduces a noun clause that is the subject or object of another sentence. As in Set 3, a noun clause is another kind of subordinate clause.

<u>That</u>   we depend on the sun's energy   is obvious.
CM
NOUN CLAUSE/SUBJECT

2. This clause marker is different from those in Set 3. Information words are for statements about the UNKNOWN. A complementizer is used for statements of FACT.

   a. Statement about the UNKNOWN
   At the age of 5, Einstein was wondering <u>how</u> a compass worked.

   b. Statement of FACT
   Later in life, he learned <u>that</u> a compass worked magnetically.

3. When the noun clause is an object, *that* may be deleted.
   Later in life, he learned a compass worked magnetically.

D. Phrase

1. A PHRASE is a set of words that:

   a. does not have both a subject and verb; and
   b. is not correct by itself.

   Katherine Anne Porter is known   <u>for her stories about women.</u>
   PHRASE

2. NOUN PHRASES and VERB PHRASES are important on the TOEFL in three cases:

   a. Problems of Word Order

   Auroras occur in   <u>the earth's magnetic field.</u>
   NOUN PHRASE

   Asia   <u>has always been considered</u>   civilization's source.
   VERB PHRASE

   b. Problems of Parallel Structure

   Three-dimensional art includes jewelry and   <u>sculpture.</u>
   NOUN PHRASE

   Scientists pose questions and   <u>gather evidence.</u>
   VERB PHRASE

   c. Appositive Forms

   The Mississippi,   <u>America's widest river,</u>   is 2,000 miles long.
   NOUN PHRASE

3. Two kinds of phrases begin with phrase markers (PMs):

   a. PREPOSITIONAL PHRASES

   <u>With</u>   the breakdown of ozone,   humans face a higher risk of cancer.
   PM
   PREPOSITIONAL PHRASE

The disintegration <u>of</u> the nuclear family   continues to occur.
                    PM
PREPOSITIONAL PHRASE

b. PARTICIPIAL PHRASES

Planes   <u>traveling</u>   at the speed of sound   create sonic booms.
            PM
PRESENT PARTICIPIAL PHRASE

Hieroglyphics   <u>written</u>   on the walls of caves   are valuable.
                  PM
PAST PARTICIPIAL PHRASE

4. Participial phrases come from relative clauses that have been reduced.

Planes   (wh<u>ich are</u>) <u>traveling</u>   at the speed of sound create sonic booms.
              ACTIVE

Hieroglyphics   (wh<u>ich were</u>) <u>written</u>   on the walls of caves are valuable.
                    PASSIVE

This is important to know when you have to decide whether to use a present participle or a past participle.

5. Appositive noun phrases, prepositional phrases, and participial phrases often separate subjects from verbs. One of the problems in Part B involves a lack of agreement between subjects and verbs, either in number or in gender. The problem is difficult to identify if a phrase separates the subject and the verb.

Word Forms

A. *Countable and Uncountable Nouns*

1. A COUNTABLE noun is something that can be counted. A countable noun can be singular or plural. To make a plural form, you add -*s* or -*es* to a noun.

nest/nests   crime/crimes   tax/taxes   quiz/quizzes

2. Some words have special spelling rules for making the plural (such as the last example above). However, the TOEFL does not test your knowledge of these rules.

3. An UNCOUNTABLE noun is something that cannot be counted. It is not divided into separate units. Some common examples:

water	information	homework	coffee	money	fruit
advice	equipment	mathematics	news	politics	oil

4. Some uncountable nouns are abstract (that is, they refer to ideas or concepts).

freedom   love   hatred   liberty   death

5. Some uncountable nouns can be made countable when they refer to specific instances or different kinds.

Americans have many *liberties.*
A major earthquake can cause many *deaths.*
The trading company imports *coffees* from all over the world.
The government instituted a quarantine on foreign *fruits.*

B. *Suffixes*

1. The grammatical form of a word must correspond to its FUNCTION in a sentence. A word may have several forms related to each other in meaning but used differently in grammar. Compare the following:

Noun	Verb	Adjective	Adverb
consideration	to consider	considerable	considerably
repetition	to repeat	repated	repeatedly
satire	to satirize	satirical	satirically

2. Below are some of the common suffixes that indicate grammatical form in a sentence.

   a. A NOUN formed from a verb:

-tion, -ion	creation, impression	(act or condition of)
-ment	development, shipment	(act of)
-ant	servant, consultant	(one who)
-er, -or	teacher, actor	(one who)

   b. A NOUN formed from a scientific term:

-ology	biology, psychology	(study of)
-ist	biologist, chemist	(one who)

   c. An ADJECTIVE formed from a verb or noun:

-ive	reflective, active, impressive
-ic	deterministic, energetic
-ent	different, convenient
-al	technical, comical
-able	considerable

   d. An ADVERB formed from an adjective:

-ly	quickly, faintly

   e. A VERB formed from an adjective or noun:

-fy	clarify, terrify
-ize	sensitize, revolutionize

   f. An ABSTRACT NOUN formed from an adjective:

-ness	happiness, politeness

Common Preposition Combinations

A. Adjective/Preposition Combinations

to be aware of
to be capable of
to be conscious of
to be different from
to be equal to
to be inferior to
to be prior to
to be similar to
to be superior to

B. Verb/Preposition Combinations

to accustom to/to be accustomed to
to acquaint with/to be acquainted with
to agree with/to agree to
to approve of
to be ashamed of
to base on/to be based on
to believe in
to care for/to care about
to compare with/to compare to
to be composed of
to be comprised of
to be concerned with/to be concerned about
to consist of
to correspond to/to correspond with
to cover with/to be covered with
to dedicate to/to be dedicated to
to derive from/to be derived from
to devote to/to be devoted to
to differ from
to be disappointed in/to be disappointed with
to distinguish between
to be done with
to engage in/to be engaged in
to finish with/to be finished with
to interest in/to be interested in
to interfere with
to involve in/to be involved in
to be known for
to be made of/to be made from
to be opposed to
to prepare for/to be prepared for
to refer to
to be reflected in
to relate to/to be related to
to result from/to result in
to be satisfied with
to tire of/to be tired of/to be tired from
to worry about/to be worried about

VOCABULARY AND READING APPENDIX

Ways to Improve Your Reading Ability and Vocabulary

- The only way to improve your ability to read efficiently is to read as much as you can in English. You won't improve if you don't practice often. Here are some suggestions:

  1. Read material from newspapers and magazines that is academic in nature. Read a variety of material on different subjects.

  2. Read as quickly as possible for general understanding. Do not stop to check words in the dictionary. Accept the fact that there will be many words you can't comprehend.

  3. As you read, pay attention to the main idea of each paragraph and the entire article.

  4. Try to express important ideas using other English words. It is very important to develop this skill of paraphrasing.

- In order to develop your knowledge of English vocabulary, you should follow these suggestions:

  1. Keep lists of new vocabulary, especially those which are academic in nature. Study these lists regularly until you have learned the words.

  2. FLASHCARDS are better than lists. Flashcards are small pieces of firm paper (like index cards), which contain:

     a. the vocabulary word (in English only) on the FRONT, possibly with an example.
     b. the definition on the BACK, with the part of grammar.

Front of Card	**Back of Card**
melancholy Mary felt melancholy at home by herself.	sad, gloomy (adjective)

You should change the order of the flashcards each time you study a set of them. Also, you should separate the difficult words from the easier ones and study them more often.

  3. Pay special attention to idiomatic expressions, mainly two- and three-part verbs, which are often tested. Some common forms are given in the Listening Appendix.

  4. Use an English/English dictionary for vocabulary study, NOT one based on your native language. Native-language dictionaries will often mislead you about the proper meaning of a word in a certain context.

Word Analysis

A. Prefixes

Prefix	Definition	Example
a-	not, not having	atypical, atheism
ante-	before	antecedent
anti-	against	antipathy, antisocial
bene-	well	benefit, benefactor
bi-	two	bicycle, binary
by-	secondary	byproduct
circum-	around	circumnavigate
co-, com-, col-	together, with	cooperate, combine, collect
contra-	against	contradict
de-	away	deflect, defend
dia-	through, across	diameter, dialogue
dis-	not	disassociate, dislike
epi-	over, outer	epicenter
in-, im-, ir-, il-	not	infinity, impossible, irresponsible, illegal
in-, im-	in	install, import
inter-	between	international, interact
intro-, intra-	inside	introduction, intrastate
micro-	small	microscope
mis-	badly, mistakenly	misinform, mistake
mono-	one, alone	monologue, monogamy
multi-	many	multimillionaire
poly-	many	polygamy, polysyllabic
post-	after	postpone
pre-	before, prior	predict, prejudice
re-	again, back	return, reaffirm
retro-	backward	retrospect
sub-	under, below	subterranean, subtract
syn-	same, together	synonym, synthesis
trans-	across	transportation
tri-	three	triangle, triad
un-	not	unknown, unusual

B. Stems

Stem	Definition	Example
-auto-	self	automatic, automobile
-bio-	life	biology, autobiography
-capit-	head	capital, decapitate
-ced-	move, go	precede, recede
-chron-	time	chronology, synchronic
-corp-	body	corpse, corporation
-cycle-	circle	bicycle, recycle
-derm-	skin	dermatologist, epiderm
-dic-, -dict-	speak, say	predict, dictionary
-duc-	lead	reduce, conducive
-fact-	make, do	manufacture
-flect-	bend	reflect, deflection
-geo-	earth	geography
-graph-, -gram-	write, writing	biography, grammar

Stem	Definition	Example
-hetero-	different	heterogenous
-homo-	same	homogenized
-hydr-	water	dehydrate, hydrogen
-log-, -logy-	study	biology
-manu-	(by) hand	manual, manufacture
-meter-	measure	thermometer
-mit-, -miss-	send	transmit, remission
-mort-	death	mortician
-onym-	name	synonym
-pathy-	feeling	sympathy, antipathy
-phil-	love	anthrophile
-phon-	sound	phonograph
-port-	carry	report, transport
-psych-	mind	psychology
-scop-	see	telescope
-scrib-	write	scribble, inscription
-secut-	follow	consecutive
-spect-	look at	inspection, spectacle
-spir-	breath	respiration, inspire
-soph-	wise	philosophy
-tele-	far	telescope
-terra-	earth	terrain
-theo-, -the-	god	theology, atheism
-therm-	heat	thermometer
-vene-, -vent-	come	convene, prevention
-ver-	true	verify

APPENDIX D

COMPLETE TOEFL TEST

SECTION 1
LISTENING COMPREHENSION

This section tests your understanding of spoken English. It is divided into three parts.

Part A

Directions: In Part A, you will hear a short statement. This statement is spoken just once. It is not written for you, so you must listen carefully to understand its meaning.

After you hear a statement, you will read four possible answers. You must choose the answer that is CLOSEST IN MEANING to the statement you hear. You will then mark the correct answer on your answer sheet.

Example I

You will hear:

You will read: (A) Tom's friend was all right.
(B) Tom and his friend had a long argument.
(C) Tom glued the end to the light.
(D) Tom spent the night alone.

You heard, "Tom argued with his friend all night." Sentence (B), "Tom and his friend had a long argument," has the closest meaning. You should mark (B) on your answer sheet.

Example II

You will hear:

You will read: (A) Can you help me review the exam?
(B) What time is the test?
(C) I don't have time to bring the test.
(D) Can I go to the test right now?

You heard, "Do you have time to go over the test with me?" Sentence (A), "Can you help me review the exam?" has the closest meaning. You should mark (A) on your answer sheet.

GO ON TO THE NEXT PAGE ➤

1. (A) You should go alone.
   (B) Let's go together.
   (C) I like going there.
   (D) He will go with you.

2. (A) What kind of person is he?
   (B) Everybody is kind to him.
   (C) How did everybody know him?
   (D) He's a kind person.

3. (A) A lot of people made it to the business meeting.
   (B) She couldn't attend the meeting.
   (C) She made time to meet the businessman.
   (D) It was a very tiring meeting.

4. (A) The stage was closed to seating.
   (B) They sat near the front.
   (C) They weren't able to choose their seats.
   (D) The seats were old and uncomfortable.

5. (A) Wasn't it an inspiring speech?
   (B) I think the speaker was perspiring.
   (C) The speech wasn't quite as inspiring as I expected.
   (D) Don't you think the speech was boring?

6. (A) Twelve teams were involved in the project.
   (B) Half a dozen team members are new to the project.
   (C) Twelve people are being removed from the project.
   (D) About a dozen people are working on the project.

7. (A) You should put off your work until later.
   (B) You'll need a ladder to do the work.
   (C) It's not a good idea to postpone your work.
   (D) Put your work where you can get it later.

8. (A) Perhaps Frank is fixing his car.
   (B) Frank is allowed to work outside.
   (C) Frank is probably putting his car out.
   (D) Maybe Frank has finished working on his car.

9. (A) I think we have time to do it.
   (B) Your trip shouldn't take so much time.
   (C) I don't think it will be ready before your trip.
   (D) I doubt you'll have time for your trip.

10. (A) She knows what to do with her money.
    (B) She has acquired a great deal of money.
    (C) She needs more money to do what she wants.
    (D) She doesn't think she's rich enough yet.

11. (A) Terry's brother is leaving in two days.
    (B) Terry is unable to visit her brother today.
    (C) Terry and her brother are coming to visit in a couple of days.
    (D) Terry's brother will arrive within two days.

12. (A) Did the mistake fool you?
    (B) He's made that mistake many times.
    (C) He forgot to take the food out of the cooler.
    (D) It was quite a foolish mistake he made.

GO ON TO THE NEXT PAGE

13. (A) He doesn't have to repeat the assignment.
    (B) The paper is a very necessary one.
    (C) He got over 80 percent on his report.
    (D) He failed to get the necessary score again.

14. (A) I'd rather not have any coffee.
    (B) Coffee sounds best to me.
    (C) I'd rather have anything but coffee.
    (D) It's a rather good cup of coffee, isn't it?

15. (A) Her concepts are considered very innovative.
    (B) The field was built according to new design standards.
    (C) A new sign is standing in the field.
    (D) She set high standards for herself.

16. (A) You'll love what I give you.
    (B) Do you want to take it now?
    (C) I'm sure you'll enjoy it very much.
    (D) Mr. Lovik took it from me.

17. (A) The physicians' efforts to revive the patient were successful.
    (B) The physicist worked patiently to develop a new strain of fruit.
    (C) The physicians were unable to save the patient's life.
    (D) The politicians worked hard to approve the new law in time.

18. (A) Dr. Carlson used to be district director.
    (B) Dr. Carlson has stopped serving as chief medical officer.
    (C) No one is a better district director than Dr. Carlson.
    (D) The district director hired Dr. Carlson as chief medical officer.

19. (A) Our schedule is hectic when we get together.
    (B) Because we're rarely apart, our schedules are very busy.
    (C) We have to make appointments just to see each other.
    (D) We're too busy to get together very often.

20. (A) We'll get the project back if the proposal is ready soon.
    (B) If we don't complete the presentation, we'll lose the project.
    (C) The president is ready to back the project we presented.
    (D) We'll have to start the project before the presentation is done.

GO ON TO THE NEXT PAGE

Part B

Directions: In Part B, you hear a short conversation between two people, followed by a question about the conversation. The conversation and question are spoken only one time, so you must listen carefully to understand what is said. After you hear the conversation and question, you will read four possible answers. You must choose the BEST answer to the question you heard. You will then mark the correct answer on your answer sheet.

Look at the following example.

You will hear:

You will read: (A) She believes they had a chance of passing.
(B) She thinks they studied enough.
(C) She wishes they could take the test again.
(D) She thinks it was a bad exam.

The conversation tells you that the woman wishes they had another chance at the exam. The best answer to the question, "What does the woman mean?" is (C), "She wishes they could take the test again." You should mark (C) on your answer sheet.

21. (A) Find out where the woman should go.
    (B) Give the woman directions to the supermarket.
    (C) Find the answer to the woman's question.
    (D) Locate his supervisor for the woman.

22. (A) The man shouldn't agree with her.
    (B) The water may be too cold to swim in.
    (C) She wants to swim some more.
    (D) She wonders why the water is so chilly.

23. (A) She didn't see what the man saw.
    (B) She doesn't have any topic to talk about.
    (C) She wants to know when he saw it.
    (D) She has no idea who he talked to.

24. (A) In a bank.
    (B) In a gift shop.
    (C) In a post office.
    (D) In a supermarket.

25. (A) He's finishing some business for Yuri.
    (B) He needs help in getting his own work done.
    (C) His business takes him all over the world.
    (D) She shouldn't be concerned about his work.

26. (A) She'd rather not go out to eat.
    (B) She wants to eat at a fast-food restaurant.
    (C) She minds having to put together a meal for him.
    (D) She'd like to eat out instead of staying home.

GO ON TO THE NEXT PAGE

160

27. (A) A repairman.
    (B) A shopper.
    (C) A delivery man.
    (D) A store clerk.

28. (A) She met someone who can pay the bills.
    (B) She billed her new roommate for the suit.
    (C) She hasn't found a suitable roommate yet.
    (D) She's looking for someone who can lend her money.

29. (A) What Fred asked her to do.
    (B) Why Fred quit school.
    (C) When Fred started giving study lessons.
    (D) How Fred is able to beat everyone.

30. (A) All his courses are demanding.
    (B) He isn't having much trouble with his classes.
    (C) The biology class is not demanding at all.
    (D) He thinks they should ask for easier classwork.

31. (A) He wants to spend a long time at the zoo.
    (B) He doesn't like to go to the zoo.
    (C) He's been to the zoo many times.
    (D) He wants to visit the zoo with her.

32. (A) The work has exhausted him.
    (B) He wants her to repeat what she said.
    (C) The work never tires him out.
    (D) He bets that he can keep doing it.

33. (A) She can start the work on Monday.
    (B) She prefers working on the report alone.
    (C) She expects the report to be done before Monday.
    (D) She needs help completing the work.

34. (A) She thinks that Aaron wears strange clothes.
    (B) She finds Aaron's sense of humor enjoyable.
    (C) She thinks that the clothing has a strange smell to it.
    (D) Aaron's clothing appeals to her.

35. (A) She's feeling normal again.
    (B) She's hoping for better weather.
    (C) She doesn't feel so well.
    (D) She'll feel better in a few days.

GO ON TO THE NEXT PAGE

Part C

Directions: In Part C, you will hear some talks and conversations. Each talk or conversation is followed by some questions. The conversations or talks and the questions about them are spoken only one time, so you must listen carefully. After you hear each question, you will read four possible answers. You must choose the BEST answer to the question. You will then mark the correct answer on your answer sheet.

Listen to this sample talk.

You will hear:

Now look at the following example.

You will hear:

You will read: (A) A new student.
(B) A university professor.
(C) The head of the Counseling Center.
(D) A department secretary.

The question, "Who is the speaker?" is the best answered by (C), "The head of the Counseling Center." This is the answer you should choose.

Now look at the next example.

You will hear:

You will read: (A) To welcome new students to the university.
(B) To change the counseling services.
(C) To take advantage of the students.
(D) To inform new students of counseling services.

The question, "What is the speaker's main responsibility?" is best answered by (D), "To inform new students of counseling services." This is the answer you should choose.

36. (A) For three-quarters of an hour.
(B) Since early in the morning.
(C) For a couple of hours.
(D) Since the noon hour.

37. (A) To get an application form.
(B) To register his car.
(C) To sign up for a special seminar.
(D) To choose his classes.

GO ON TO THE NEXT PAGE

38. (A) Early summer.
    (B) The end of fall.
    (C) Midwinter.
    (D) The beginning of spring.

39. (A) Choose her classes later.
    (B) Go shopping for clothes.
    (C) Wait for him at the car.
    (D) Check the oil and air.

40. (A) At the man's apartment.
    (B) At their present location.
    (C) In the parking lot.
    (D) At the service station.

41. (A) A university administrator.
    (B) A physical facilities supervisor.
    (C) A communications company trainer.
    (D) A telephone technician.

42. (A) To solve telecommunications problems on- and off-campus.
    (B) To notify university administrators of new telecommunications regulations.
    (C) To train campus personnel on the use of a new communications system.
    (D) To design and develop a new computerized data storage system.

43. (A) A lack of extension numbers.
    (B) Inadequate technical assistance.
    (C) Too many complicated features.
    (D) Slow speed of service.

44. (A) Sophisticated telephone jacks.
    (B) Call waiting.
    (C) Automatic memory redial.
    (D) Quicker response time.

45. (A) Until a new system can be found.
    (B) For only a few years.
    (C) Between two and three months.
    (D) For a number of decades.

46. (A) In a stationery store.
    (B) In an art supply store.
    (C) In a copy center.
    (D) In a campus bookstore.

47. (A) Get 40 pieces of paper.
    (B) Copy and bind 40 pages.
    (C) Buy a class packet.
    (D) Cash a check.

48. (A) A colored kind.
    (B) A standard stock.
    (C) An expensive type.
    (D) A cheap recycled brand.

49. (A) In several minutes.
    (B) Early next morning.
    (C) In a half hour.
    (D) Later in the afternoon.

50. (A) She thinks it is a mistake.
    (B) She expected it to be less.
    (C) She wants to pay by credit card.
    (D) She thought it would be more.

THIS IS THE END OF SECTION 1.

STOP STOP STOP STOP STOP STOP STOP

SECTION 2
STRUCTURE AND WRITTEN EXPRESSION

Time—25 minutes

This section tests your ability to identify appropriate forms of formal written English. There are two parts to this section.

<u>Directions:</u> Questions 1–15 contain sentences that are incomplete in some way. You choose the ONE answer that completes each sentence properly.

Example I

The horizon appears to be curved when viewed _____ a high place.

(A) with
(B) from
(C) on
(D) out of

The sentence should read, "The horizon appears to be curved when viewed from a high place." Therefore, (B) is the correct answer.

Example II

_____ the meaning of vocabulary from context is an important skill.

(A) Determining
(B) Having determined
(C) It is determined
(D) Determination

The sentence should read, "Determining the meaning of vocabulary from context is an important skill." Therefore, (A) is the correct answer.

Now begin work on the questions.

1. The Canterbury Tales, _____ by English poet Geoffrey Chaucer, are a fine example of Middle English.

   (A) a story set of
   (B) as sets of stories
   (C) a set of stories
   (D) stories in a set

2. Albert Camus, a French journalist who won the 1957 Nobel prize for literature, _____ about individual freedoms and alienation from society.

   (A) and wrote passionately
   (B) writing passionately
   (C) he wrote passionately
   (D) wrote passionately

GO ON TO THE NEXT PAGE

3. Cardiac arrest occurs _____ heart muscles stop beating during a heart attack or after a severe accident.

   (A) when
   (B) in that
   (C) although
   (D) due to

4. Harvard University is one of the oldest _____ private educational institutions in the United States.

   (A) but rich
   (B) and richest
   (C) yet richer
   (D) and the rich

5. It is not clear _____ the form of humor known as a limerick started.

   (A) if
   (B) how
   (C) which
   (D) whenever

6. _____ only U.S. state that is not situated on the mainland of North America.

   (A) Hawaii, the
   (B) It is Hawaii the
   (C) Hawaii is the
   (D) Because Hawaii is the

7. Hannibal, the military genius of Carthage, was best known _____ the mountains of the Pyrénnées and Alps with elephants.

   (A) as crossed
   (B) for crossing
   (C) with the crossing of
   (D) having crossed

8. Of all types of health maintenance organizations, _____.

   (A) the most common being a prepaid group practice plan
   (B) a prepaid group practice plan was commonly
   (C) there is the most common a prepaid group practice plan
   (D) a prepaid group practice plan is the most common

9. The strong beam of light from a lighthouse is used by sailors _____

   (A) to determining their location
   (B) for determination their location
   (C) in determining their location
   (D) while determined their location

10. _____ travels 5.8 trillion miles in one year has been scientifically proven.

   (A) That light
   (B) Light
   (C) For light to
   (D) When light

11. A caricature is a form of art involving a picture _____ the physical nature of an important person.

    (A) exaggerated
    (B) that exaggerates
    (C) having exaggerated
    (D) exaggerating that

12. Resources such as factories or equipment used to produce goods and services are _____ as capital.

    (A) referred
    (B) referring in
    (C) referred to
    (D) being referred

13. In the 1830s railroads _____ canals as the most important means of transportation in the United States.

    (A) replacing by
    (B) were replaced
    (C) was replacing
    (D) replaced

14. The human body acquires nutrients from food particles _____ the blood.

    (A) carrying
    (B) carried in
    (C) carrying by
    (D) has carried

15. Rarely _____ primitive tribes of Africa, Asia, and the Pacific Islands practice cannibalism today.

    (A) have
    (B) are
    (C) do
    (D) is it

GO ON TO THE NEXT PAGE

166

Directions: Questions 16–40 contain sentences that are incorrect in some way. You choose the one underlined part that is wrong.

Example I

Particles of salt dissolved in water retains their salinity.
   A   B   C   D

The sentence should read, "Particles of salt dissolved in water retain their salinity." Therefore, (C) is the proper choice.

Example II

The emissions from a diesel-powered automobile are not as dangerous as
      A   B

that from a gasoline-powered vehicle.
C   D

The sentence should read, "The emissions from a diesel-powered automobile are not as dangerous as those from a gasoline-powered vehicle." Therefore, (C) is the proper choice.

Now begin work on the questions.

16. The Persian poet Hafiz wrote a popular collecting of 700 poems called a
    A   B   C   D
divan.

17. All the necessary ingredient for the survival of plants and animals are
   A   B   C
found within a habitat.
   D

18. The first person to sign Declaration of Independence in 1776 was John
        A   B   C   D
Hancock.

19. The heart is a large hollow muscle that pumps blood out the body.
    A   B   C   D

20. Hares resemble rabbits yet having longer and larger legs and ears than their
               A   B   C   D
cousins.

21. The field of linguistic concerns itself with the analysis and use of language.
   A   B   C   D

22. A migraine, considered to be the bad kind of headache, can cause nausea in
         A   B   C
the most extreme cases.
   D

GO ON TO THE NEXT PAGE

23. A carnival is a form of amusement involving games, rides, shows,
        A   B
    and exhibiting in an outdoor area.
        C   D

24. Carbohydrates, which include all sugars and starches, are the source main of
                  A   B   C
    energy for the body.
        D

25. The alphabet invented about 1500 B.C. by Semitic people inhabiting the
                 A   B   C   D
    Middle East.

26. The importance of historical perspective in the understanding of human
                   A   B
    culture was a primary concern of the well-known German philosophy George
                C   D
    Hegel.

27. Advances in computer graphics have brought on a new era in the field of
      A   B   C
    cartoon animated.
      D

28. Since the early 1900s Luther Burbank bred a spineless variety of cactus that
      A   B   C
    can be eaten as food.
      D

29. Manuscript writing consists of letters written straight up and down and not
               A   B   C
    connecting to each other.
      D

30. Calamity Jane was a famous American frontierswoman who was adept with
            A   B   C
    handling a horse and rifle.
              D

31. Calculus, one of the most important mathematical areas, are used for
           A   B   C
    measuring changing quantities of speed and distance.
      D

32. Lacquer is a shiny substance that protects the surface of metals, woods, and
          A   B   C
    porcelain from wear or tear.
            D

33. In large amounts, caffeine can induce nervousness and caused loss of sleep.
      A   B   C   D

34. Latin America comprises of that part of the Western Hemisphere south of
             A   B   C   D
    the United States.

35. Latium, the area of ancient Italy after which the Latin language was named,
           A   B   C
    it was part of the Roman Empire.
      D

GO ON TO THE NEXT PAGE

36. <u>Leather is</u> the <u>durable and long-lasting</u> material <u>obtained from</u> the <u>skin of</u>
       A   B   C   D
    animals.

37. <u>Contrary to</u> popular belief, the hump of a camel <u>contains fatty</u> tissue only
      A   B
    <u>and has</u> no water inside <u>of them</u>.
      C   D

38. <u>The domed</u> cathedral Hagia Sophia in Constantinople <u>is a</u> fine <u>example of</u>
      A   B   C
    the Byzantine style <u>of architectural</u>.
                        D

39. The process <u>of replacing</u> lost <u>parts of</u> bodies or <u>doing new</u> forms <u>is called</u>
                A   B   C   D
    regeneration.

40. <u>In practical</u> all <u>societies</u>, females <u>live longer</u> than their <u>male counterparts</u>.
      A   B   C   D

THIS IS THE END OF SECTION 2.

SECTION 3
VOCABULARY AND READING COMPREHENSION

Time—45 minutes

This section tests your understanding of written English. It is divided into two parts.

<u>Directions:</u> In questions 1–30 each sentence has a word or phrase underlined. Below each sentence are four choices, and you must select the one that MOST CLOSELY MEANS THE SAME AS the underlined word.

Example

Meteorologists use balloons to <u>forecast</u> weather patterns.

(A) cause
(B) predict
(C) create
(D) test

(B) is the correct answer because the word "predict" most closely means "forecast."

Now begin work on the questions.

1. The Code of Hammurabi in ancient Babylonia had great influence on the civilizations of <u>nearly</u> all Near Eastern countries.

   (A) clearly
   (B) quite
   (C) closely
   (D) almost

2. One-third of the Earth's surface area of <u>approximately</u> 197 million square miles is devoted to farming.

   (A) totally
   (B) largely
   (C) exactly
   (D) roughly

3. One of the oldest forms of folk art is handicraft, the <u>creation</u> of objects with the hands.

   (A) invention
   (B) activity
   (C) hobby
   (D) elevation

4. Indication that cannibalism was once a religious <u>practice</u> dates back almost 500,000 years.

   (A) custom
   (B) assignment
   (C) recital
   (D) business

GO ON TO THE NEXT PAGE

5. Coffee contains the odorless, <u>bitter</u> substance caffeine, which acts as a stimulant to the human heart and nervous system.

   (A) sweetened
   (B) acrid
   (C) delicious
   (D) pure

6. Electrical conductors such as copper and aluminum need to be <u>insulated</u> from the possible signal interference of other conductors.

   (A) connected
   (B) realigned
   (C) protected
   (D) redistributed

7. Alex Haley spent 12 years <u>investigating</u> his family history from Africa in the 1700s to the present day.

   (A) developing
   (B) researching
   (C) categorizing
   (D) declaring

8. An heir is defined as the legal <u>beneficiary</u> of the money or property of a person who has died without leaving a will.

   (A) relative
   (B) associate
   (C) recipient
   (D) ancestor

9. John Gower's *Confessio Amantis* is <u>an exemplary</u> poem combining Biblical, medieval, and mythological stories to explore the problems of romantic love.

   (A) a detailed
   (B) a model
   (C) a resolute
   (D) a simple

10. The two basic principles of aerodynamics, lift and drag, are <u>applied to</u> the design of all airplanes, vehicles, and buildings.

    (A) registered in
    (B) combined with
    (C) relegated to
    (D) employed in

11. The poetry of T.S. Eliot was known for its complicated style and <u>extensive</u> use of symbolism.

    (A) widespread
    (B) accurate
    (C) limited
    (D) lengthened

12. The sharp bristles of a cactus prevent desert animals in search of moisture from <u>devouring</u> it.

    (A) destroying
    (B) consuming
    (C) cultivating
    (D) manipulating

GO ON TO THE NEXT PAGE ➤

13. The theory of laissez-faire economics holds that government should not interfere with competition in an open market.

   (A) a prescribed
   (B) a free
   (C) a spacious
   (D) a balanced

14. A wide range of conditions, including injury, infection, and allergic reaction, can bring on a headache.

   (A) induce
   (B) alleviate
   (C) negate
   (D) foment

15. The inherent freedom of economic choice within the capitalist system promotes competition in the production of goods and services.

   (A) chronic
   (B) regulated
   (C) intrinsic
   (D) novel

16. Robert Heinlein, a well-known American science fiction writer, made his stories plausible by explaining the nature of future societies in great detail.

   (A) credible
   (B) entertaining
   (C) unrealistic
   (D) zealous

17. Latex, the milklike juice given off by plants and trees of the sapodilla family, is used in producing gums and rubbers.

   (A) covered
   (B) emitted
   (C) attached
   (D) delivered

18. The breakdown of the ozone layer surrounding the Earth correlates with the increased occurrence of skin cancer.

   (A) movement
   (B) deterioration
   (C) failure
   (D) itemization

19. The Mississippi River has always played an indispensable role in trade and commerce through the nation's heartland.

   (A) a developmental
   (B) a thorough
   (C) an elevated
   (D) an essential

20. The action of water vapor and carbon dioxide in keeping heat created by sunlight from escaping back into space is appropriately named the greenhouse effect.

   (A) incorrectly
   (B) usually
   (C) deliberately
   (D) suitably

GO ON TO THE NEXT PAGE ▶

21. Halloween customs developed from ancient religious <u>festivals</u> that occurred the day before All Saints' Day.

    (A) celebrations
    (B) services
    (C) documents
    (D) traditions

22. The work of Frank Lloyd Wright, one of America's greatest architects, has <u>enduring</u> beauty for those who appreciate his unique style.

    (A) captive
    (B) lasting
    (C) regressing
    (D) serene

23. Many lawsuits are resolved through <u>settlement</u> prior to court due to the effort and expense involved in trial.

    (A) debate
    (B) amelioration
    (C) dismissal
    (D) compromise

24. The writ of habeas corpus is a basic personal freedom under American law that compels police authorities to justify <u>incarcerating</u> an individual.

    (A) releasing
    (B) suspecting
    (C) restraining
    (D) imprisoning

25. The time between submission of <u>a manuscript</u> to a publisher and eventual publication can sometimes take several years.

    (A) a prologue
    (B) a composition
    (C) an addendum
    (D) an essay

26. Helen Hayes, one of America's <u>outstanding</u> actresses, won an Academy Award for the first film performance of her long and distinguished career.

    (A) preeminent
    (B) charming
    (C) reclusive
    (D) profound

27. Cursive writing involves letters <u>angled</u> to one side or another and connected together.

    (A) supported
    (B) regulated
    (C) slanted
    (D) relegated

28. Prehistoric man drew simplified <u>representations</u> called pictographs on cave walls to depict common articles and ideas.

    (A) outlines
    (B) images
    (C) coordinates
    (D) illusions

GO ON TO THE NEXT PAGE

29. Northern carpetbaggers were viewed by Southerners as <u>opportunistic</u> intruders seeking wealth and political power in the wake of the Civil War.

(A) generous
(B) self-serving
(C) invading
(D) decisive

30. Hairdressing, the art of caring for the hair, has existed as a <u>bona fide</u> profession since the 1700s.

(A) dominant
(B) dubious
(C) casual
(D) genuine

GO ON TO THE NEXT PAGE ➤

Directions: In this part you will read passages on various topics and answer questions about them. Some answers to the questions are directly stated, while others are only suggested.

Read the following passage:

The pituitary gland, one of the body's key organs, generates a number of hormones that help control body function. Sometimes known as the hypophysis, the gland has two main parts—the anterior lobe and the posterior lobe. It is about the size of a pea and is located near the center of the skull.

Example I

According to the passage, what is another name for the pituitary gland?

(A) The anterior lobe
(B) The hormone
(C) The hypophysis
(D) The posterior lobe

The passage states that the pituitary gland is also known as the hypophysis. Therefore, the correct answer is (C).

Example II

It can be inferred from the passage that the pituitary gland is

(A) quite small
(B) divided into several parts
(C) very large
(D) composed of a number of hormones

The passage states that the pituitary gland is about the size of a pea, which suggests that it is quite small. The correct answer is (A).

Now begin work on the questions.

GO ON TO THE NEXT PAGE

Questions 31–35

The United States population is growing older. In 1987, 12 percent of Americans were 65 years old or older, compared with 8 percent in 1950. Population experts at the U.S. Bureau of the Census expect this percentage to continue to rise gradually, reaching 14 percent in 2010, then to skyrocket

(5) during the next 20 years, reaching 21 percent by 2030. This "graying of America" has generated concerns about whether the best really is yet to be, about how well off tomorrow's elderly will be. There also are questions about the impact of an aging population on the rest of society.

The graying of America has two causes. First, advances in medical care

(10) have enabled people to live longer. In the United States in 1900, the average life expectancy at birth was 47.3 years. By 1985, the latest year for which figures are available, it has climbed to 74.7 years.

Second, the U.S. birthrate rose in the mid-1900s, interrupting a long, slow decline. A dramatic increase occurred during this brief rise. From 1945

(15) to 1947, the rate jumped from 20.4 births for every 1,000 people to 26.6. In 1957, the birthrate was still high—25.3—but then began to decline. The birthrate dropped to the 1933 level of 18.4 in 1966, and by 1985, was 15.7. Most experts see little change in the downward trend of the birthrate in the foreseeable future.

31. What is the author's main purpose in the passage?

(A) To bring attention to the needs of the elderly
(B) To contrast birthrates and life expectancy rates
(C) To explain how and why the American population is aging
(D) To show the percentages of age groups in the general population

32. During which period of time will the percentage of Americans 65 years old or older increase the most?

(A) 1970–1990
(B) 1990–2010
(C) 2010–2030
(D) 2030–2050

33. In the first paragraph, the phrase "the graying of America" refers to

(A) the uncertainty of the future for older Americans
(B) the effects of population on the health of the elderly
(C) statistics released by the U.S. Bureau of the Census
(D) the increasing number of elderly people in the population

GO ON TO THE NEXT PAGE

34. About how long did it take the birthrate to return to the 1933 level?

    (A) 20 years
    (B) 30 years
    (C) 40 years
    (D) 50 years

35. Which of the following conclusions about the birthrate is supported by the passage?

    (A) The long-range decline in the birthrate will continue in the next century.
    (B) Another dramatic increase in the birthrate will occur before the 21st century.
    (C) The birthrate will continue to vary greatly.
    (D) An increase in the birthrate depends mainly on advances in medical care.

GO ON TO THE NEXT PAGE ▶

177

Questions 36–41

In countries having democratic forms of government, political parties compete in open elections for the right to run the government. The primary functions of parties include nominating suitable candidates for public office, selecting issues for public debate and persuading persons who

(5)   have registered to vote to elect its slate. Party leaders are also responsible for raising money to finance costly political campaigns.

Once elected, party officials try to implement the policies of their party in the operation of government. If the party has just taken over control of the government, smooth operation of the system and implementation of

(10) policy might take months to achieve. In the case of a party that retains its hold on the government through reelection, the clear mandate of the people normally results in a flurry of new laws that can influence the social and economic climate of a country for years.

The primary function of the party or parties not elected is to question

(15) the policies of the party in control. The minority parties publicize what they consider deficiencies in the majority party's program and offer voters an alternative. This healthy opposition serves as a check against the excesses of power seen in one-party systems.

36. Which of the following is the best title for the passage?

(A) Democratic Forms of Government
(B) The Roles of Political Parties
(C) Election of Government Officials
(D) Functions of Political Campaigns

37. According to the passage, elections in a democracy are

(A) run by party officials
(B) organized by potential candidates
(C) vulnerable to the excesses of power
(D) open to individuals who have signed up to vote

38. Which of the following is NOT mentioned as one of the functions of political parties?

(A) Raising funds for financing government elections
(B) Choosing candidates to run for office
(C) Deciding on issues for public discussion
(D) Convincing people to vote for its slate of candidates

GO ON TO THE NEXT PAGE

39. According to the passage, a party reelected to power

   (A) may require months to recover from the effects of a difficult election contest
   (B) can have great impact on the future health and welfare of a nation
   (C) attacks the deficiencies of the minority party's program
   (D) often suffers the excesses in power of one-party systems

40. It can be inferred from the passage that a democratic country

   (A) endures none of the disadvantages of a one-party system
   (B) must constantly regulate the activities of its political parties
   (C) maintains at least two political parties acting in opposition
   (D) benefits from the fund-raising activities of political parties

41. According to the passage, what is the role of a political party NOT in control of the government?

   (A) It serves as an alternative to the ruling party and its policies.
   (B) It helps to implement governmental policy until the next election.
   (C) It questions the legality of the ruling party's actions.
   (D) It follows the people's mandate by legislating new laws.

GO ON TO THE NEXT PAGE

Questions 42–48

The phenomenon of lightning has been a source of danger and mystery through the centuries, and only recently have scientists begun to understand its true nature. We know now that lightning is a huge electrical spark caused by the interaction of electrically charged particles in the
(5)   atmosphere. During a thunderstorm, heavy particles take on a negative charge and fall to the bottom of clouds, while particles holding a positive charge rise to the top. Lightning results when energy flows between the two types of charges.

What is still not understood is the process by which particles become
(10) electrically charged. Most scientists believe that a cloud's light, rising moisture and tiny pieces of ice collide with hail and other heavy, falling particles. The collision may cause these elements to take on either a positive or negative charge.

The most feared form of lightning is that which strikes the ground in
(15) one or more electrical discharges called strokes. Any one of these strokes is capable of causing death, destroying property, or igniting fires. It is interesting to note that the bright flash of light produced by a stroke actually occurs as the discharge returns to the sky and not as it descends towards the ground. This return stroke heats surrounding air and causes it
(20) to expand, thus producing a wave of pressure called thunder.

42. Which of the following is the best title for the passage?

(A) A Dangerous Phenomena
(B) Atmospheric Occurrences
(C) The Nature of Lightning
(D) Scientific Mysteries

43. The passage states that lightning is

(A) a recent source of mystery
(B) a giant spark of electricity
(C) an electrically charged particle
(D) a type of thunderstorm

44. According to the passage, lightning results from

(A) a flow of energy between positive and negative charges
(B) discharges in a heavy thunderstorm
(C) the rising and falling of heavy particles
(D) great amounts of electricity in the atmosphere

45. It can be inferred that positively charged particles are

(A) the primary cause of lightning
(B) found only during thunderstorms
(C) not involved in the production of lightning
(D) lighter than negatively charged ones

GO ON TO THE NEXT PAGE

46. According to the passage, particles become electrically charged when

(A) light, ascending matter collides with heavy, falling elements
(B) energy flows between light and heavy charged particles
(C) heavy particles rise to the tops of clouds
(D) a return stroke heats the surrounding air and causes it to expand

47. The paragraph following this passage most likely discusses

(A) the nature of thunder
(B) other types of lightning
(C) the dangerous effects of electrical discharges
(D) another natural phenomenon

48. The author implies that most people believe they observe lightning

(A) as being slower than the speed of light
(B) only in conjunction with the sound of thunder
(C) as it rushes down to strike the earth
(D) in the form of strokes released in the atmosphere

GO ON TO THE NEXT PAGE

Questions 49–53

Abraham Lincoln, the 16th president of the United States, was one of the truly great men of all time. He preserved the American Union during the Civil War and proved to the world that democracy can be a lasting form of government. Lincoln's Gettysburg Address, and many of his other
(5) speeches and writings, are classic statements of democratic beliefs and goals.

Lincoln's outstanding asset was insight. Lincoln realized at the beginning of the Civil War that the Union must be saved. The United States was the only important democracy in the world. Lincoln knew that self-
(10) government would be proved a failure if the nation could be destroyed by a minority of its own people. He determined that the nation, and democracy, would not be destroyed.

Lincoln's second greatest asset was his ability to express his convictions so clearly, and with such force, that millions of Americans made them their
(15) own. Lincoln would have been surprised that some of his speeches came to be honored as great literature. He sought only to be understood, and to convince.

Lincoln's third great source of strength was his iron will. The Civil War had to be carried on until the Union was restored. At times, people in the
(20) North wavered in this purpose. Lincoln never doubted that in the end, right would make might, and the North would triumph. His unyielding faith in victory helped to win victory.

49. According to the passage, what was the Gettysburg Address?

(A) A declaration of war against the South
(B) A famous talk by Lincoln on democratic principles
(C) One of the essays on government written by Lincoln
(D) Lincoln's speech at his inauguration

50. According to the passage, what was Abraham Lincoln's greatest strength?

(A) The ability to see the true nature of a situation
(B) The capacity to express his views in public
(C) His success in becoming president of the United States
(D) The impact of his speeches and writings

GO ON TO THE NEXT PAGE

51. The author probably feels that Lincoln

(A) was at times too stubborn for his own good
(B) never fully realized the importance of self-government
(C) was as great a writer as he was a politician
(D) was single-handedly responsible for saving the Union

52. The passage would most likely be found in a textbook on which of the following subjects?

(A) Historical literature
(B) Public administration
(C) The Civil War
(D) Political science

53. According to the passage, Abraham Lincoln believed that the North

(A) would quickly triumph over the minority of people trying to destroy the Union
(B) would achieve victory through the moral power of its cause
(C) did not have the strength to continue the Civil War for a long time
(D) could waver in its purpose and lose the struggle

GO ON TO THE NEXT PAGE

Questions 54–60

Radiocarbon is a radioactive isotope with an atomic weight of 14, which makes it heavier than ordinary carbon. Radiocarbon forms when cosmic rays, or high-energy atomic particles, collide with the Earth's atmosphere. This collision causes atoms to disintegrate into smaller

(5) elements. One of these elements, the neutron, smashes into the nuclei of nitrogen atoms and, in the process of being absorbed into the nuclei, causes a proton element to be released. In this manner a nitrogen atom turns into a radiocarbon atom.

Radiocarbon is found in all living matter. For every trillion molecules

(10) of carbon dioxide gas, the atmosphere contains about one radiocarbon atom. Plants assimilate radiocarbon from carbon dioxide in the air, and humans absorb it mainly from food made from plants.

Radiocarbon is very useful in establishing the age of old objects. The technique of radiocarbon dating was developed by an American chemist,

(15) William F. Libby, in the late 1940s. He discovered that radioactive carbon atoms decay at a regular rate over long periods of time. After about 5,700 years, half the radiocarbon in dead material disappears. After 11,400 years, half the remaining material is gone. Using his method, archeologists have been able to determine the age of objects up to 50,000 years old.

54. The main topic of this passage is

(A) the weight of radioactive isotopes
(B) differences between radioactive carbon and regular carbon
(C) the origin and uses of radiocarbon isotopes
(D) forms of cosmic rays

55. According to the passage, what happens when atomic particles strike the Earth's outer layer?

(A) Atoms break down into smaller components.
(B) Radiocarbon becomes heavier.
(C) They are absorbed by all living matter.
(D) Protons are released into the atmosphere.

56. According to the passage, radiocarbon results when

(A) it is heavier than regular carbon
(B) atomic particles escape the Earth's atmosphere
(C) a neutron hits the nucleus of a carbon atom
(D) a nitrogen atom absorbs a neutron and releases a proton

57. According to the passage, how do people primarily take in radiocarbon?

(A) From animal food
(B) By breathing the air
(C) From carbon dioxide molecules
(D) From edible vegetation

GO ON TO THE NEXT PAGE

58. Compared to carbon dioxide gas, radiocarbon

    (A) is a rare element
    (B) is found in equal quantities
    (C) has unusual properties
    (D) is a very common element

59. In line 11, the word "assimilate" could best be replaced by which of the following?

    (A) produce
    (B) transfer
    (C) reduce
    (D) absorb

60. It can be inferred from the passage that an object that is 11,400 years old

    (A) contains half its original radiocarbon content
    (B) has no radiocarbon left
    (C) has about a quarter of its radiocarbon remaining
    (D) has less than an eighth of its initial radiocarbon matter

THIS IS THE END OF SECTION 3.

Listening Transcript, Explanations, and Answers for Complete TOEFL Test

SECTION 1
LISTENING COMPREHENSION

Part A

Example I   Tom argued with his friend all night.
Example II   Do you have time to go over the test with me?

1. I'd like to go with you.
2. How kind he is to everybody!
3. She was too tired to make it to the meeting.
4. They chose seats close to the stage.
5. The speech was quite inspiring, don't you think?
6. The project involves a team of about 12 people.
7. If you put off your work, you'll regret it later.
8. Frank may be outside working on his car.
9. I doubt that it'll be done in time for your trip.
10. Charlene Jackson has more money than she knows what to do with.
11. Terry's brother will come to visit her within the next couple of days.
12. Only a fool like him would make that kind of mistake.
13. It's not necessary for him to write the paper over.
14. There isn't anything I'd rather have than a good cup of coffee.
15. Sally's design concepts have set new standards for her field.
16. Take it from me—you'll love it!
17. The physicians worked hard to revive the patient, but over time their efforts proved fruitless.
18. Dr. Carlson was chief medical officer before becoming district director.
19. We rarely have time to be together because our schedules are so hectic.
20. Unless the presentation is ready soon, we'll have to back out of the project.

Answers	1. (B)	2. (D)	3. (B)	4. (B)	5. (A)	6. (D)
	7. (C)	8. (A)	9. (C)	10. (B)	11. (D)	12. (D)
	13. (A)	14. (B)	15. (A)	16. (C)	17. (C)	18. (B)
	19. (D)	20. (B)				

Part B

Example

M: Too bad we both failed the exam. I guess we didn't study hard enough for it.
W: If only we had another chance at it.
Q: What does the woman mean?

21.   *W:* Could you please get me your supervisor? I'd like to speak with her.
      M: I'll have to find out where she is. One moment, please.
      Q: What is the man going to do?

22.   *M:* The water's a bit chilly for swimming, isn't it?
      W: I couldn't agree more!
      Q: What does the woman mean?

23. *M:* Did you see that?
    W: I haven't any idea what you're talking about.
    Q: What does the woman mean?

24. *W:* I'd like to send this package overnight, please.
    M: Certainly. That'll be $9.42.
    Q: Where does this conversation probably take place?

25. *W:* What in the world are you working on?
    M: It's really none of your business.
    Q: What does the man mean?

26. *M:* Let's eat out tonight, OK?
    W: Would you mind if I put together a quick meal here instead?
    Q: What is the woman suggesting?

27. *W:* Is it too late to go in? I just have a couple of items to get.
    M: I'm sorry, ma'am, but I've got to close up the store now.
    Q: What is the man's occupation?

28. *M:* Have you found a roommate to share your apartment?
    W: I'm still looking for someone who fits the bill.
    Q: What does the woman mean?

29. *W:* I wonder what made Fred give up his academic studies.
    M: Beats me, too. You'd better ask him yourself.
    Q: What does the woman want to know?

30. *M1:* Are you having problems with your classwork?
    M2: Not really. Biology is somewhat demanding, though.
    Q: What does the man mean?

31. *W:* Where would you like to go?
    M: I haven't been to the zoo in a long time.
    Q: What does the man mean?

32. *W:* I bet you're tired of working.
    M: You can say that again.
    Q: What does the man mean?

33. *M:* Will you be able to finish the sales report by next Monday?
    W: Not if you expect me to do it alone.
    Q: What does the woman imply?

34. *M:* Aaron certainly has a strange sense of humor.
    W: The same can be said for his taste in clothes.
    Q: What does the woman mean?

35. *M:* How are you feeling today?
    W: Oh, I've seen better days, thanks.
    Q: What does the woman mean?

Answers	21. (D)	22. (B)	23. (A)	24. (C)	25. (D)
	26. (A)	27. (D)	28. (C)	29. (B)	30. (B)
	31. (D)	32. (A)	33. (D)	34. (A)	35. (C)

Part C

Example

I'd like to welcome you to the Counseling Center. As head of the department, I am responsible for informing you, as new students, of the ways we can provide assistance. Many students do not take advantage of our academic and personal counseling services, but we are working to change that situation.

Example 1   Who is the speaker?
Example 2   What is the speaker's main responsibility?

Questions 36–40 refer to the following conversation.

M: How long have we been standing in line?
W: Oh, about 45 minutes.
M: This is ridiculous. They should use the same system in the summer as they use in the fall and spring.
W: Yeah, the line is moving rather slowly.
M: I'm sorry to put you through this. I had no idea it would take so long.
W: That's OK. I don't have anything better to do.
M: Didn't you say you wanted to go clothes shopping?
W: Yes, but that can wait.
M: Well, I was thinking that you'd better go shopping, and I'll meet you after I sign up for classes.
W: Are you sure? I don't mind waiting.
M: No, really. This couldn't take more than a couple of hours, so I can meet you back at my place around noon.
W: OK. Can I have the keys to your car?
M: Here they are.
W: Is the key to your apartment on the ring, too?
M: Yes, it is. Oh, by the way, can you put some gas in my car?
W: Sure thing. Should I check the oil and air, too?
M: Come on, stop teasing me.
W: I'm not joking. I'd be glad to.
M: No, they're OK. Thanks for offering.
W: I'm going now. See you later, and good luck.
M: Yeah, I'll need it. I probably won't get what I want.
W: You may be surprised!

36. How long have the man and the woman been standing there?
37. Why is the man waiting in line?
38. What time of the year is it?
39. What does the man suggest the woman do?
40. Where are the man and the woman going to meet later?

Questions 41–45 refer to the following talk.

The purpose of this session is to train you on the use of the university's new, computerized communications system, which will entirely replace the present operation within two months. We have now completed the second of three stages in the project. All campus buildings and most off-campus sites have already been wired, and the main switching unit is in place. The rest of the wiring and installation of the telephone jacks will be completed by the end of this month. You won't notice much change in the most common uses of the equipment, but you will have a host of new features at your disposal. These include automatic memory redial and call-forwarding features. We'll be talking about these later in the session. I'm proud to say that the system is the result of a lengthy, thorough analysis of the on-campus needs of the administration, faculty, and students and will easily carry us through the next few decades. The most serious problem plaguing the current setup—that is, a shortage of extension numbers—will never again prevent the university from meeting its telecommunications needs. And of course our company will remain under contract with the university to provide ongoing technical assistance. We don't expect any major problems, but we'll be there just in case.

41. Who is the speaker?
42. What is the purpose of the session?
43. What has been the most serious problem with the present system?
44. Which of the following is mentioned as a feature of the new system?
45. How long will the new system probably be in use?

Questions 46–50 refer to the following conversation.

M: Hi. How can I help you?
W: I'd like to have these 40 pages done.
M: Sure. Would you like them back-to-back?
W: Is it cheaper to have it done that way?
M: No, the cost is the same.
W: Then I'd like them on separate sheets.
M: Any preference as to the paper quality?
W: No, just the regular kind. Oh, I'd also like to have it bound.
M: Fine. What color would you like on the cover?
W: What are the choices?
M: We have blue, green, red, yellow, and pink.
W: I think I'll get blue.
M: OK, we'll have it done in about ten minutes. That comes to $5.20.
W: Good. I was afraid it would be more, and I only have seven dollars.
M: By the way, we also accept credit cards.
W: That's good to know. I'll pay cash this time, though.

46. Where does this conversation probably take place?
47. What does the woman want to do?
48. What kind of paper does the woman want?
49. When can the woman pick the material up?
50. How does the woman react to the cost?

Answers	36. (A)	37. (D)	38. (A)	39. (B)	40. (A)
	41. (C)	42. (C)	43. (A)	44. (C)	45. (D)
	46. (C)	47. (B)	48. (B)	49. (A)	50. (D)

SECTION 2
STRUCTURE AND WRITTEN EXPRESSION

Structure

1. (C). The appositive form is incomplete. A noun phrase is needed in the blank.
2. (D). The main clause is incomplete. The main verb and an adverb are missing.
3. (A). The clause marker is missing. (C) is a clause marker, but it does not create the proper relationship between the two clauses.
4. (B). A coordinating conjunction and superlative form are needed.
5. (B). The information word *how* is needed. The clause marker *if* (A) is correct grammatically, but does not fit in this context.
6. (C). The main clause is incomplete. The main subject and verb, as well as an article, are missing.

7. (B). The past participle *known* is often used with the preposition *for*, which can be followed by a participle form.
8. (D). The entire main clause is missing. (D) is the only answer that has the appropriate wording.
9. (C). The prepositional phrase, which includes a gerund form, is missing.
10. (A). A sentence of fact acting as subject of another sentence should be introduced by *that*.
11. (B). The subordinate clause is incomplete. The clause marker and verb are needed.
12. (C). A passive verb form is appropriate, and *refer* occurs with the preposition *to*.
13. (D). *Railroads* is the subject and *canals* is the object. An active verb form is needed in this case.
14. (B). The correct answer is a reduced form of "food particles that are carried in the blood..." A past participle form is used here.
15. (C). After an initial negative term, a question form should be used. Since the verb *practice* is a simple present tense form, (C) is correct.

Written Expression

16. (C). The form of the noun is wrong. The correct answer is *popular collection*.
17. (B). The noun form *ingredient* is countable and should be plural. The correct answer is *ingredients*.
18. (B). A definite article is needed. The correct answer is *the Declaration*.
19. (D). The choice of preposition is wrong. The correct answer is *throughout*.
20. (A). This is a problem of parallel structure involving the verbs *resemble* and *have*. The correct answer is *yet have*.
21. (B). The main verb is *concerns*, so the preceding word cannot be the adjective form *linguistic*. The correct answer is *linguistics*, a singular noun form.
22. (B). A superlative adjective form should be used. The correct answer is *the worst*.
23. (C). This is a problem of parallel structure involving nouns. The correct answer is *and exhibits*.
24. (C). This is a problem in word order. The correct answer is *main source*. Note that (B) is correct when referring to different types of sugar.
25. (A). A passive verb is needed; the clue is the phrase *by Semitic people*. The correct answer is *was invented*.
26. (D). The noun should refer to a person, not a field of study. The correct answer is *philosopher*.
27. (D). The form of the noun is inappropriate. The correct answer is *cartoon animation*.
28. (A). The verb *bred* indicates past time. The correct answer is *in the*.
29. (D). This is a problem of parallel structure involving past participle forms. The correct answer is *connected to*.
30. (C). The choice of preposition is wrong. The correct answer is *at*.
31. (C). The main subject is singular, so the verb must also be singular. The correct answer is *is used*.
32. (D). This is an idiomatic form. The correct answer is *wear and tear*.
33. (C). This is a problem of parallel structure involving the verb forms *induce* and *cause*. The correct answer is *cause*.
34. (A). There are two possible solutions to this problem. Either a passive verb form should be used, or the preposition should be omitted. The two possible correct answers are *is comprised of* or *comprises*.
35. (D). The use of *Latium* and *it* creates a double subject. The correct answer is *was*.
36. (B). *Long-lasting* means the same as *durable*, so this is a problem of redundancy. One form or the other should be removed.
37. (D). The pronoun must agree in number with the preceding noun it refers to. The correct answer is *of it*, referring to the hump of a camel.
38. (D). A noun form is needed. The correct answer is *of architecture*.

39. (C). The choice of word is inappropriate. *Make*, not *do*, should be used. The correct answer is *making new*.
40. (A). An adverb form should be used. The correct answer is *in practically*.

SECTION 3
VOCABULARY AND READING COMPREHENSION

Vocabulary

1. (D). *Near* means *close*, but the adverb forms of these words do not have the same meaning.
2. (D).
3. (A).
4. (A). The context indicates this answer because a custom (practice) develops over time.
5. (B).
6. (C).
7. (B).
8. (C). The context suggests that an heir receives wealth. *Recipient* is the noun form of the verb "to receive."
9. (B). *Exemplary* is the adjective form of "example." An example often serves as a model.
10. (D).
11. (A).
12. (B). The context suggests that animals eat or drink (consume) in order to find moisture.
13. (B).
14. (A). *Bring on* is an idiomatic form meaning *cause* or *induce*.
15. (C).
16. (A).
17. (B). *Give off* is an idiom meaning *produce* or *emit*.
18. (B).
19. (D). *In*-means "not" and -*dispens*- means "throw away." If something is indispensable, it is very important (*essential*).
20. (D).
21. (A).
22. (B).The stem -*dur*- involves time, which suggests (B).
23. (D).
24. (D). The prefixes *in*- and *im*- both mean "into."
25. (B).
26. (A).
27. (C). The context (*to one side or another*) suggests this answer.
28. (B).
29. (B).
30. (D).

Reading Comprehension

Questions 31–35

31. Type: Main Idea
    Key terms: main purpose
    Answer: (C)

    Lines 1 and 9 clearly indicate the main idea. The other answers are all specific details.

32. Type: Detail
    Key terms: which period, percentage, increase
    Answer: (C)

    The answer is found in lines 4 and 5.

33. Type: Detail
    Key terms: graying of America
    Answer: (D)

    This phrase is used following a discussion of the increase in the percentage of the elderly in the population.

34. Type: Detail
    Key terms: how long, birthrate, 1933 level
    Answer: (B)

    The answer is in lines 16 and 17 (1966–1933 = about 30 years).

35. Type: Inference
    Key terms: birthrate
    Answer: (A)

    This conclusion is supported by the first and last sentences of the third paragraph.

Questions 36–41

36. Type: Main Idea
    Key terms: best title
    Answer: (B)

    (B) best describes the overall purpose of the passage. (A) is too general, and (C) and (D) are too specific.

37. Type: Detail
    Key terms: elections
    Answer: (D)

    The answer is in lines 4 and 5 (*persuading persons who have registered to vote to elect its slate*).

38. Type: Detail
    Key terms: NOT mentioned, functions, political parties
    Answer: (A)

    The other answers are mentioned in lines 3–5. Political parties fund their own political campaigns (lines 5 and 6), while the government finances the election.

39. Type: Detail
    Key terms: party reelected
    Answer: (B)

    The answer is in lines 10–13.

40. Type: Inference
    Key terms: democratic country
    Answer: (C)

This answer is suggested in lines 1 and 2, as well as lines 14 and 15.

41. Type: Detail
    Key terms: role, NOT in control
    Answer: (A)

    The answer is in lines 14 and 15.

Questions 42–48

42. Type: Main Idea
    Key terms: best title
    Answer: (C)

    (C) accurately describes the overall purpose of the passage. (A) is mentioned in line 1 as part of the introduction to the passage, but it is not the main idea (that is, the passage is not devoted only to the dangers of lightning). (B) and (D) are too general.

43. Type: Detail
    Key terms: lightning
    Answer: (B)

    The answer is in lines 3 and 4.

44. Type: Detail
    Key terms: results from
    Answer: (A)

    The answer is in lines 7 and 8.

45. Type: Inference
    Key terms: positively charged particles
    Answer: (D)

    This answer can be inferred from lines 5–7. Heavy particles become negative charges, so positive charges must be lighter.

46. Type: Detail
    Key terms: electrically charged when
    Answer: (A)

    This answer is in lines 10–13.

47. Type: Inference
    Key terms: paragraph following
    Answer: (B)

    This answer is suggested by the first sentence of the third paragraph (line 14). (A) may seem possible, but the last sentence of the third paragraph has already explained the nature of thunder.

    NOTE: The answer for this kind of question usually comes from the first sentence of the last paragraph, and NOT the last sentence of the passage.

48. Type: Inference
    Key terms: observe lightning
    Answer: (C)

This answer can be inferred from lines 17–19. The expression *interesting to note* suggests that the explanation that follows runs contrary to popular opinion.

Questions 49–53

49. Type: Detail
    Key terms: Gettysburg Address
    Answer: (B)

    The answer is in lines 4–6. An *address* (stress on the first syllable) is a formal speech.

50. Type: Detail
    Key terms: greatest strength
    Answer: (A)

    Greatest strength means *outstanding asset* (line 7). *Insight* (line 7) is the ability to see the true nature of a situation. The paragraph then gives an example of this insight.

51. Type: Inference
    Key terms: probably feels
    Answer: (C)

    This answer is supported by lines 1 and 2 along with lines 15 and 16.

52. Type: Inference
    Key terms: likely found, subjects
    Answer: (D)

    The study of American presidents is undertaken within the field of political science.

53. Type: Detail
    Key terms: Lincoln believed, North
    Answer: (B)

    The answer is found in lines 20 and 21. Answer (B) is a paraphrase of the expression *right would make might*.

Questions 54–60

54. Type: Main Idea
    Key terms: main topic
    Answer: (C)

    (C) accurately identifies the overall purpose of the passage. (A) and (B) are too specific, and (D) is too general.

55. Type: Detail
    Key terms: atomic particles, Earth's outer layer
    Answer: (A)

    The answer is in lines 3 and 4. *Disintegrate* means *break down*.

56. Type: Detail
Key terms: results when
Answer: (D)

The answer is in lines 5–8.

57. Type: Detail
Key terms: people, take in
Answer: (D)

The answer is in line 12. *Edible vegetation* indicates *food made from plants*.

58. Type: Detail
Key terms: carbon dioxide
Answer: (A)

This answer is indicated by lines 9–11. *One in every trillion* means that something is very rare.

59. Type: Detail
Key terms: line 11, assimilate, replaced
Answer: (D)

Line 12 provides the correct answer (*absorb*).

60. Type: Inference
Key terms: 11,400 years old
Answer: (C)

This answer can be inferred from lines 16–18. Half of a half is a quarter.